I0088741

The Black Belt Book of Life

Secrets of a Martial Arts Master

Kiado-Ryu Grandmaster
Richard Andrew King

© by Richard Andrew King
Published by Richard King Publications
PO Box 3621
Laguna Hills, CA 92654

No part of this publication may be reproduced or transmitted in any form or by any means, electronic or mechanical, including photocopy, recording or any information storage and retrieval system now known or to be invented without permission in writing from the publisher, except by a reviewer who wishes to quote brief passages in connection with a review written for inclusion in a magazine, newspaper, online article or broadcast. Contact Richard King Publications, PO Box 3621, Laguna Hills, CA 92654.

This book and its information contains copyrighted material, trademarks, and other proprietary information. You may not modify, publish, transmit, participate in the transfer or sale of, create derivative works of, or in any way exploit, in whole or in part, any Proprietary or other Material in this work.

Library of Congress Cataloging-in-Publication Data

King, Richard Andrew
The Black Belt Book of Life
ISBN: 978-0-931872-10-5

Date of Publication: 12 December 2009

DEDICATION

To the Brotherhood of the

Karate Institute of America,

its Black Belts, students, parents,

and loyal supporters who believe in its

principles, ideals, values and ethics and

who have contributed to the rich history and

legacy of the Kiado-Ryu martial arts system.

SPECIAL THANKS

A special thanks to Tashia R. Peterman,

graphic artist and photographer,

for her wonderful cover art.

(www.tashiasphotography.com)

A SPECIAL DEDICATION

to

Vince "Sly" Weber,

41st Black Belt of the Kiado-Ryu,

whose beautiful spirit has been returned to God.

Sly was a one-of-a-kind human being:

loving husband, father, friend, teacher;

a man with a heart of gold and the spirit of a warrior.

His life touched us all but his indomitable goodness will live

with us, the Kiado-Ryu and the Karate Institute of America

forever.

6

ACKNOWLEDGMENTS

To Dave "Rugman" Sampson, the 42nd Black Belt of the Kiado-Ryu, for his undying loyalty, devotion, friendship, unparalleled expertise, genuine sense of humor, endless generosity and humility. Rugman has been critically instrumental in establishing and cementing the legacy of the Kiado-Ryu and the Karate Institute of America throughout its existence in ways too many to mention but for which we are truly and eternally grateful.

To Jeff "Boa" Norman, the 51st Black Belt of the Kiado-Ryu, for his immense generosity, kindness and undying support in insuring the entire student body of the Karate Institute of America was securely anchored in its own dojo, taking it out of the rain and giving it a beautiful environment and workout facility.

To Chris "Growler" Grau, Kiado-Ryu Black Belt #36, for his generosity, devotion and professional expertise in promoting and furthering the legacy and history of the Karate Institute of America and the Kiado-Ryu system of martial arts through developing, maintaining and serving as webmaster of our Kiado-Ryu website.

CONTACT
Richard Andrew King
PO Box 3621 Laguna Hills, CA 92654-3621
www.RichardKing.net www.Kiado-Ryu.com

The Black Belt Book of Life
Secrets of a Martial Arts Master

Table of Contents

Author's Introduction

I began my martial arts journey in March of 1968. It was the first step of an empowering, enlightening, fulfilling, meaningful, joyous, endless pilgrimage of personal integration for which I am, and will always be, eternally grateful. I'm sure many of you who are reading this book feel the same way, especially if martial arts has become for you, as it has for me, not simply an extracurricular activity, but a way of life. In fact, I feel extremely blessed to have been able to make it a profession since 1979, when I founded the Karate Institute of America in Orange County, California, and developed the Kiado-Ryu system of martial arts.

It is difficult to put into words the extreme value that martial arts training has had on my life. It is truly a discipline that integrates the body, mind and spirit like nothing else. There is no sport, no activity, nothing that incorporates, captivates and demands every component of our being more than the warrior arts, arts in which we engage not so much the slaying of external adversaries but rather the adversaries of our own life - the demons, dragons, weaknesses, faults, failings and shortcomings we all bring into this world.

From first gasp to final exhalation we must struggle through this life for, as Twentieth Century Saint, Sawan Singh stated, *This world is the plane of struggle.* His grandson, Perfect Master, Charan Singh, reiterated this truth by declaring, *In this world there is nothing but strife, struggle and conflict.* Gautama the Buddha commented, *Existence is suffering.* Therefore, if any soul is to manage his existence well from cradle to grave, he must learn to be a courageous warrior, to heartily engage the battle of life, to keep fighting and moving forward - regardless of all the bumps, lumps, bruises, falls and failings on the journey until, through undaunted and relentless persistence, victory is assured - victory realized in becoming a realized soul. Martial arts training is, indeed, a powerful strategy in the pursuit of triumph.

This book is not about physical fighting strategies and tactics. It is about concepts and principles we learn through martial arts training that can help us in the struggle of life, in the journey to conquer ourselves and gain the golden ring of our own completeness, for in the end, a true Black Belt should be a realized soul who, having engaged the enemy - himself - finds himself at the end of the journey . . . triumphant.

Yours in the Arts,

Richard Andrew King
Founder & Grandmaster
The Karate Institute of America
and the Kiado-Ryu System of Martial Arts

#1
Martial Arts Is Life

Let your hands

give wings to your mind,

that you may find

an ever-greater Power of Life,

a Power preserving the

sanctity of your soul

and illuminating the radiance

of your Perfection.

If you believe that martial arts training is designed to enable you to beat up on others, I would suggest you look within yourself to assess why you feel a need to impose yourself on others. I would then suggest you look more deeply within yourself to determine the true meaning of martial arts training, that training that guides you upward to the higher ideals of nobility and self-mastery, for in the end the true test of our skill and achievement lies not in our mastery of others, but in mastery of ourselves. As the famed Pythagoras so eloquently stated, *No man is free who cannot control himself,* and most certainly, martial arts training teaches us to control ourselves before anything else.

Martial Arts is Life. Everything we do when we train has some correlation to life outside the milieu of our training ground - be that ground the floor of a dojo, studio, gym, backyard, living room, meadow, forest, or mountain top. It doesn't matter where we study. The thing of importance is that we do study, that we engage ourselves in the process of learning and developing our character, courage, strength, will, devotion, discipline, dedication, concentration, commitment, consistency, focus, flexibility, respect for ourselves and others; patience, tolerance, tenderness, kindness, poise, calm, centeredness, self-control and the integration of our body, mind and spirit. The list of attributes is endless, but everything mentioned above is a life principle and they are all an integral part of martial arts training and education.

Martial arts is an internal path, not an external path, although ostensibly it appears to be external. Often in our training we are pitted against an opponent to hone and test our skills, but in reality our real opponent is life, and he is a very worthy adversary. When he attacks us, as he does often with great tenacity, we need skills to defeat him and advance ourselves onward and upward. Yet, his purpose is not to destroy but sculpt, to strengthen and make us worthy of greater achievements.

Therefore, to get the most from our martial arts training, my suggestion is that every time we train we see such training as life training, not simply martial arts training, because in the final analysis martial arts is not just an extracurricular activity. Martial Arts is Life.

#2

Your Life,
Your Responsibility

In your life journey from breath to death,

replete with all its possibility,

never forget . . . this is *Your Life*,

and it most surely is *Your Responsibility*.

Work out your own salvation.

Do not depend on others.

Buddha

[400 BCE]

I blame not another.

I blame my own karmas.

Guru Nanak

[15th/16th Century]

You are responsible for yourself.

You are not responsible for the world.

Saint Charan Singh

[20th Century]

Our world is quickly being transformed from one of independence to dependence. Everywhere we look someone is making or attempting to make someone else responsible for them and their lives. These souls have lost sight of their dignity and self-respect, choosing rather to rely on someone else to take care of them rather than they taking care of their own selves, their own lives.

This condition of looking to others for one's well-being is not the way of the natural world. It is the way of the unnatural world, and through the unnatural order of things a person loses the great gift of learning to stand on his own two feet and be counted as one who, in the end, although perhaps bloodied, crippled, worn, torn, abused and bruised, challenged life himself and ultimately emerged victorious. In the private battle of life there is dignity. In the private battle of life there is great nobility. In the private battle of life there is courage, and definitely emerging from the private battle of life is the tranquility of an undaunted and indomitable spirit.

From moment one in martial arts training the focus is on personal growth through one's individual efforts. The warrior journey is not one of looking to others for one's success. It is a solo journey of looking to, and relying upon, the self. It is a path forcing the soul to stand on its own two feet and be accountable for its life in all aspects. For the warrior, the path is not about holding hands. It is about holding and manifesting a vision of self-doing, self-worth and personal dignity.

Take kumite for example. Kumite is sparring, i.e., controlled combat. It is the pitting of ourselves against another, and it is done *alone*. It is not done while holding hands with another or looking to another to protect us from our opponent. When learning to fight in such a controlled way, we learn step by step to solve our own problems, to take blows, to give them, to face and overcome our fears, to do for ourselves while disallowing others to do for us. By learning to stand up and fight our own fights, we become skilled, strong, courageous, confident, self-reliant, composed, whole. We learn that the outcome of the fight rests solely within us and everything we bring to the challenge. We learn that the outcome of the struggle is our responsibility, not someone else's. We learn, ultimately, that through this process of combat our life is, indeed, our life, and it is most assuredly, our responsibility.

This principle of self-responsibility is not only life-enriching, it is life-preserving and never more clear than in the case of a beautiful young martial arts student about five feet tall and maybe ninety-five pounds dripping wet. Before going off to college she reached the rank of brown belt, a noteworthy accomplishment.

After arriving at college, this vibrant young woman was walking down one of the main roadways in the city. Without warning, a car pulled up beside her, stopped, and out jumped several guys who attacked her and tried to pull her into the car. With an understanding that her life was her responsibility, she went into aggressive self-defense mode. She fought back - one young, tiny college coed against male assailants all intent on rape or worse. She kicked, she scratched, she punched, she blocked, she refused to be taken and transported against her will. Eventually, the bad guys decided she was too much trouble and not worth their nefarious efforts. They got back into their vehicle and fled the scene. She survived. Hurrah for her! How did she survive? She survived because she knew the fundamental principle of life is that *It's Your Life; It's Your Responsibility.*

#3

Our Accomplishments Are Not Our Life. Our Life Is Our Accomplishment

Attainment

As we progress and seek success
in its full embodied raiment,
Accomplishments are not our life,
our Life is our Attainment.

Possessions will not follow us
when we move beyond the grave.
Monies will be left behind
in the banks where they were saved.

Accolades and laurels
may, with some history, rest,
but none of these material things
will help us pass the Test.

Therefore, we should cogitate
on how our time is spent, for our
Accomplishments are not our life,
our Life is our Attainment.

How we live from day to day
at the center of our core,
is highly more important
than the things with which we score.

Ethics, morals, honesty,
purity, love and trust,
although not greatly popular,
are the things which go with us

when we move beyond this life
and the shadow of the veil,
for they will be the substance
of our life, its times and tale.

And they will be the basis
of the Judgment God will make
when He outlines the blueprint
of the future path we take.

Thus, prudent it would be to know
in quest of the Ascent,
Accomplishments are not our life,
our Life is our Attainment.

How often in life do we get sidetracked with achieving all kinds of worldly things - name, fame, celebrity, riches, power, status, lands, titles, properties and on and on? The list of things we set out to accomplish in this life is endless, but the germane issue is that all worldly attainments are exactly that, worldly. Sound a little esoteric? Perhaps, but it's true.

Life is energy. It can neither be created nor destroyed. When the intrinsic energy that is "us" is separated from its physical form, that energy will go on. The physical body will not. So of what value are all the worldly accomplishments that enslave us? We can't take anything of this world with us when we go except our spirit and its consciousness. Therefore, it is our spirit and its development that a wise man would do well to cultivate. To involve oneself in the pursuit of things associated only with this life is a waste of life and the worst of all investments.

Martial arts training principally focuses on one thing - the development of our spirit. This is arguably its greatest gift to those of us who become its students. In martial arts training we learn discipline, balance, concentration, courage, self-responsibility and practically an endless litany of spirit-based principles which become infused into every fiber of our consciousness. These gifts go with us when we depart this world because they are us, quite unlike all the worldly things and titles we normally devote our life to which are all as fleeting as a candle flame in a hurricane. In the end, these worldly treasures betray their owners, ultimately rendering them losers, not winners.

How do we measure life? Here's a thought: think of the richest person on the face of the earth. When that person dies, for all their worldly wealth, riches, fame, name, celebrity, power and authority, when it comes time for them to exhale their last breath, they will not be able to buy one . . . single . . .more . . . breath. How priceless then is one breath? The answer . . . priceless.

Given this thought, a definition of success is here offered and it is this: success in life will not be measured until the first moment after the last breath is exhaled. It is then the individual will realize how successful or unsuccessful he was in life because his spirit will either rise or fall as it moves forward to the next phase of its existence. Seldom does the spirit stay at the same level. One sobering thought to keep in mind is from a Saint of the 15th and 16th Centuries named Guru Nanak who said, *Ranks of this world will not be recognized in the next.*

Therefore, place a high value on your training as a martial artist. It is not a waste of time. In fact, it is an extremely wise expenditure of time, effort and energy. Look deeply into what you are really learning. Is it simply how to defend yourself? How to beat someone up? A method to stay in shape, to commingle with others, to socialize? Or does martial arts training offer greater gifts than those normally perceived? Even if you achieve the coveted rank of Black Belt through a worthy system, is that in itself just a worldly accomplishment? Frankly, no, for reasons stated above. Whether we are martial artists or not, the main thing to remember is that *Our accomplishments are not our life; our life is our accomplishment.*

#4

Balance Is Primary

Of all life's skills

with which to carry,

remember this . . .

Balance is Primary!

Anyone can teeter-totter

but not everyone can balance.

Anonymous

Man always travels along precipices.

His truest obligation is to keep his balance.

Pope John Paul II

The best and safest thing is to keep a balance in your life,

acknowledge the great powers around us and in us.

If you can do that, and live that way,

you are really a wise man.

Euripides

[480-406BC]

Arguably, the greatest of life's skills is balance. With it, life is potentially harmonious, productive, meaningful. Without it, life is extremely challenging, bringing a torrent of angst, confusion, destruction, non-productivity and unhappiness. When the teeter-totter is constantly going up and down, how can stability be maintained? It can't, and where there is no stability, there is, axiomatically, instability and all of its attending issues and problems.

The principle of balance is echoed in Aristotle's *Golden Mean,* the desirable midpoint between two extremes. Although less clear in its understanding, Confucius expounded what he called *The Doctrine of the Mean.* Both of these timeless philosophers lived three hundred and two hundred years BC, Aristotle predating Confucius by approximately one hundred years.

Yet, their message rings true throughout time: balance is primary and without balance the hope for a productive, fulfilling and meaningful life is compromised, if not totally negated.

Although the physical aspect of balance is readily apparent in martial arts training, it is no less critical to develop emotional, psychological and spiritual balance as well. If any one of these facets is missing in our character make-up, there will be a chink in our armor potentially creating problems for us in life. Therefore, it is vitally important that we constantly work to achieve a state of balance in all things.

It is not easy to achieve balance. Try standing on one leg for any length of time. It's difficult. Stand on an inflated rubber dome, disk or gymnastics balance beam and the task becomes even more difficult. Still need more challenge? Try these balance exercises with your eyes closed. As time in the balance position increases, the challenge becomes practically overwhelming, resulting in falling off the mark. If standing on one foot is not challenging enough, try a handstand on the ground. Then proceed to parallel bars, gymnastic rings or the balance beam again. Hardly an easy skill. Even the best gymnast cannot hold his balance point for more than a few minutes on any given apparatus.

It is through these exercises that we understand balance is a dynamic and active process, not a passive one. Our mind, muscles, tendons, ligaments and joints are all continually moving to keep us centered. We learn from such exercises that balance is truly a difficult state to maintain, not just in a physical sense, but also in a mental, emotional and spiritual sense as well. Thus, leading a successful life becomes a continual struggle and is definitely not a passive activity but an energetic and constantly dynamic one.

One of the main ingredients of balance is concentration, a focus of our attention on the alignments that keep all of our body parts in sync in the physical realm. When standing on one foot, for example, the key to balance is to insure that our head, shoulders, hips, supporting knee, ankle, foot and our body's center line are properly aligned. Thus, balance becomes a problem of alignment. To simply try and balance on one foot doesn't do us much good because there's no concrete understanding of what creates balance. But when we focus on the alignment of the parts responsible for the balance, the probability of success increases dramatically.

It is no different when we are working to keep our life in balance except that we have to expand our focus to include our mind, heart, spirit, health, finances, relationships, etc. - all aspects that are necessary to life and which, if in the proper alignment, help insure a successful life through the principle of balance. Once we lose our focus, our alignment goes and so our balance goes and with it the peace that would be generated from a life of equanimity.

It is difficult to maintain balance in this world because it is based on a bipolar structure - the interplay of opposites. The ancient Yin/Yang symbol of the Chinese Tao beautifully depicts this ebb and flow of opposite energies: positive/negative; light/dark; male/female; hard/soft; day/night; up/down; hot/cold; happy/sad; good/bad and so forth. In this world the great cosmic pendulum is forever swinging back and forth from one polarity to the other and in such a constantly changing environment it is difficult to maintain balance, which is why mystics call this earth the "plane of struggle," and why martial arts practice focuses on teaching and learning the virtue of balance. And what is the key to balance? Concentration.

#5

Concentration Is The First Key

Balance is Primary.

This we see,

but in the struggle of life

Concentration Is The

very *First Key.*

Concentration is the secret of strength.

Ralph Waldo Emerson

Balance is primary, no doubt. However, concentration is the first key to success in whatever we do. If we can't focus our attention directly on the task at hand, there is a pronounced risk of not succeeding at all and more poignantly, a lethal risk if confronted with a life-threatening situation.

The combat aspect of martial arts training teaches us the critical reason for having total concentration. Even in a light sparring exercise we could get severely injured if we lose our concentration for a fraction of a second. Why? Because fighting happens in a fraction of a second. For example, a well-trained attacking hand can move much faster than the human eye can see, let alone the mind perceive, assimilate, and deliver a counter strike or move. People do make mistakes in sparring no matter how controlled the format. A wrong move, an unblocked kick or hand strike, a poorly chosen angle of attack or defense or miscalculated timing can get one hurt. And this is in a controlled environment. The consequences of losing one's focus in a real situation runs the scale from injury to fatality . . . of ourselves or someone we're attempting to protect.

True story. As a case in point, one of the greatest and most gifted athletes in Kiado-Ryu history was competing in kumite [fighting] at a national tournament. The things this gentleman could do athletically were off the scale of normal athleticism. Yet, he lost his very first fight in that tournament. When I asked him, in astonishment, what happened in the fight his exact and profound words were, "I blinked." That's the reality of fighting and of life and death. Had this great athlete not blinked, not lost his concentration for an eye-blink of time, the outcome of that fight may have been much different. But it wasn't. This simple example underscores the importance of why *concentration is the first key.*

Developing this life-giving and life-saving skill of concentration is a great benefit of martial arts training because in sparring drills we learn to never lose our concentration, to remain constantly focused on our opponent, our objective. Even if we're totally concentrated on the task at hand, there is no guarantee we'll be successful, but if we lose our concentration, there's a very high level of probability we'll fail.

The Black Belt Book of Life   King

This same lesson of concentration applies also to kata - the performance of choreographed martial arts routines. It can also be applied to any performance activity, especially live performances such as singing, acting or public speaking. It's one thing to practice a routine alone in a studio, home, office, shower, the backyard, etc., but when competing in a tournament or performing on stage before a live audience or in front of a camera, losing one's concentration can be deleterious to the successful accomplishment of the task at hand. Total success demands total concentration.

Fighting or performing are obvious examples of activities in which concentration is critical, but it is no less critical in life, and a lack of proper concentration can be just as deadly. For example, assume you're perched on a cliff on one side of a thousand foot high crevasse that is a hundred feet across. Spanning this fissure is a four inch wide beam upon which you must walk to get to the other side. If you fall from this height, death is certain. You start to walk, knowing that if you make one mistake it will be your last. This is important to remember because we often think that life gives us second chances. Wrong. Life doesn't always give second chances and there are certainly no guarantees that it does. Therefore, we must be focused . . . always.

So you start walking across this four inch beam in an attempt to get to the other side. Do you dance on the beam? No. Do you make sudden moves? No. Do you jump up and down for joy? No. Do you turn around to see how far you've come? No. Do you become overwhelmed with emotional grief or ecstatic exuberance at any point in this hundred foot live-or-die scenario? You'd better not. In fact, the only thing you'd better do is keep your concentration - visually, physically, mentally, emotionally - if you want not to die. At no point while walking on this four inch beam spanning a thousand foot high, one hundred foot wide crevasse can you afford to lose your concentration. By keeping your focus you have a better chance of keeping your balance [remember, balance is primary] and become successful in your quest to get to the other side of the fissure. Lose your concentration and you die. It's as simple as that.

This is, of course, a severe example. Or is it? In life we don't traverse thousand foot high and hundred foot wide crevasses on a four inch beam, or do we? Do you drink and drive? If so, you're on this life-or-death beam. Do you drive under the influence of any mind-altering or mind-inhibiting drug? If so, you're on the beam. Do you indulge in risky sexual behavior? If so, you too are on the beam. This last question was never more tragically significant than the man who said on a primetime television talk show regarding his desire to have sex, which he had never had and through which he acquired AIDS, "I was dying to have sex, and now I'm dying because I had sex, once!" What he lost before he lost his life was his concentration on choices he should have made for his life's well-being and safety.

This example is severe, of course. Still, it underscores the need for concentration in everything we do - in our relationships, our careers, our meditations, our every day-to-day actions inside and out of the martial arts classroom. Without a doubt, if we want to be successful in anything or be kept from experiencing heartache and misery, we must remember that *concentration is the first key.*

#6

To Become Everything We Must First Become Nothing

In the game of life,

whether pauper, prince or king,

the fact remains --

To Become Everything

We Must First Become Nothing.

This is a strange statement, isn't it: *To become everything we must first become nothing*? Yet, it is true and possesses great mystic meaning. If martial arts teaches anything substantive, it is to integrate the body, mind and spirit. Nothing will help us with the integrative process more than surrendering our egos to the Great Power that exists, the Power which created and sustains us; which gives us life.

Interestingly, contemporary thought is that to become something, we must be somebody or accomplish some great thing or be some acknowledged celebrity or famous icon among the masses. Spiritual thought, which is the true basis of martial arts thought, runs contrary to this concept. Remember, *our accomplishments are not our life; our life is our accomplishment.*

Life trumps accolades. It is far better to live a life-filled life than a trophy-filled life. As the famous 1st Century Latin writer and philosopher, Publilius Syrus, commented: *God looks at the clean hands, not the full ones.*

Becoming everything by becoming nothing is like the analogy of the single drop of water and the ocean. When we exist as a single drop of water, we are separated from our source. We have limited power. We may be something, but it is a little something. However, when we merge into the ocean, we become the ocean. We lose our little identity, our ego, and reflect the Identity of All that is. We move from the separated drop of water to merging into the great ocean of life and thereby acquire its power which is infinite in relation to the "little drop of us." There is no longer separation. There is union, oneness with the power of all powers. We become complete and whole, unfettered by the issues and problems of the little self, the little identity, the little thing. Instead, by merging with the All, the Power that is, we become everything. *Therefore, to become everything, we must first become nothing.*

#7

You Must Win
The Cross

In cleansing the soul

and losing its dross,

it's axiomatic --

You Must Win The Cross.

Without recognizing the ordinances of Heaven,

it is impossible to be a superior man.

Confucius

nother way of expressing the phrase, *To become everything you must first become nothing*, is this corroborating maxim, *You Must Win the Cross.* The symbol of the cross is ancient, far antedating its use by Christianity. It also has application to martial arts.

What is the *cross* in martial arts? Actually, it's several things. The first is associated with the combat environment and its structure. The distance between fighters is referred to as the "gap." To physically engage in combat, this gap must be crossed by one or both fighters. The fighter who crosses this gap most efficiently

The Black Belt Book of Life   King

and safely is likely to be victorious in the engagement. Hence the phrase, *You Must Win the Cross* or, in other words, the *crossing*.

The second meaning of winning the cross is philosophical with tactical overtones. As discussed in the previous vignette, *To Become Everything You Must First Become Nothing*, the goal is to eliminate the individual ego by sublimating it to the Great Power or Divine Source that creates and sustains it.

In the following two part diagram, Image A [a vertical straight line] represents the self, the ego. The second, Image B, which has the appearance of a cross, represents that self, that ego, being expunged, i.e., crossed out by a horizontal line.

Image A. The Self [expressed as a vertical line]

Image B. The Eradication or "crossing out" of the Self [expressed as a cross]

It is the expunging of the self, the ego, in surrender to a greater power that is the basis of the statement, *You Must Win the Cross*.

The tactical overtones of this statement not only apply to crossing the gap between fighters, but also to the more important understanding that the successful fighter must eliminate his ego, especially as it is a function of his mind. When we fight, often we think too much. In the fiery speed of battle, however, there is not time to think. There is only time to act or react. By the time one stops to think, the fight could be over with the one who paused to think laying prostrate, never to think again.

Another tactical aspect of the phrase *You Must Win the Cross* involves not thinking that the fight is all about us. At least 50% of the fight is about the opponent. By studying him, his physical attributes, athleticism, quickness, balance, rhythm, posture, footwork, stance, weight distribution, general movement and fighting temperament, we gain insight as to how to exploit any weaknesses or chinks in his armor or fighting style. If we ignore studying him and think that the fight is all about us, we will most likely not be successful unless we get lucky. By winning the cross, i.e., by eliminating that part of our warrior-self that may think the fight is only about us and our ability, we increase our chances of victory. As the famous Chinese warlord Sun Tzu observed, to be successful in combat we must know ourselves and our opponent. This knowledge will insure victory and negate disaster.

Thus, *You Must Win the Cross* has both tactical and philosophical implications. Regarding the former, it secures victory in conflict. Regarding the latter, it allows us to grow beyond our ego and ultimately assist us in merging with that greater Power that created us, sustains us, and is the very core of our being. All high level mystics teach that in order to merge into God we must ultimately relinquish our own egos. Otherwise it is impossible to do so. Therefore, the admonition and exhortation in both fighting and life is to remember, *You Must Win the Cross*!

#8

Character Is More Important Than Victory

In a phenomenal world
with its contents illusory,
of all the triumphs
Character Is More
Important Than Victory.

The gem cannot be polished without friction.
Chinese Proverb

Only a man's character is the real criterion of worth.
Do what you feel in your heart to be right - for you'll
be criticized anyway. You'll be damned if you do,
and damned if you don't.
Eleanor Roosevelt

Character cannot be developed in ease and quiet.
Only through experience of trial and suffering can the
soul be strengthened, ambition inspired, and success achieved.
Helen Keller

It is one thing in life to be victorious in our battles, whether those battles involve internal or external opponents. Yet, one thing is clear and must never be overlooked and that is that *Character is More Important than Victory.*

Victory and defeat are opposite ends of the same continuum. Both are temporal, short lived. Furthermore, it is a fundamental law of life that when the pendulum swings one way it must, by its very nature, swing the other. Therefore, we must never be elated in victory or discouraged in defeat. Both victory and defeat are parts of the same process.

How often in life do we see victors gloat over their triumphs? How often do we likewise see losers sulk and hang their heads? Neither is commendable. What is worthy is for a person to remain balanced at all times and in all situations, realizing that character is more important than either victory or defeat.

Because of the nature of this world, people often gain victory by buying it, bribing it or stealing it. What nobility is there in such a victory? Nothing. Such a victory is nothing more than an empty illusion fueled by the fires of ego and emptiness. Anyone who would gain a victory in such a manner is no victor at all but a loser of the greatest proportions.

True story. During a fighting competition at a major national martial arts tournament, a gentleman signed up to fight in the Black Belt under 175 lb. weight division. All the other competitors voiced their objection in a mass protest because this individual was clearly over the 175 lb. weight limit. He more accurately weighed closer to 200 lbs. Tournament officials were called to the ring to assess the situation. The officials, betraying their own eyes, knowledge and experience, allowed this man to fight because he showed an entrance pass validating his weight at 175 lbs. Because of his increased mass, he won the division. He gained his victory, or did he? It was later discovered after he won that this man, so hungry to be a champion, had paid another man to weigh in for him, thus falsifying his application, which was sadly and quite unprofessionally accepted by the tournament officials. Basically, this so-called black belt was devoid of character, totally. Yet, he won, or so the record books say. With such an abuse of ethics and unprofessional conduct by the tournament hierarchy, a huge defeat was registered that day in the category of professional ethics.

Is this story rare? Unfortunately not. In all walks of life people achieve things they don't rightfully deserve because of politics, money, personal favors, nepotism and a whole host of dishonest means. So are such people who gain victory and acclaim by such devious and unethical conduct true champions? Of course not. Yet, such is the reality of life in this imperfect world. Therefore, it is critical for the ethical person to understand this unfortunate reality, not be negatively affected by it, but rather to exude a higher code of true victory in life, a code declaring that *Character is more important than victory.*

#9
Character Must
Precede Prowess

In the wisdom of time

with its messages ageless,

the pinnacle of all is that

Character Must Precede Prowess.

The first essential step to a spiritual life is character.
One may deceive one's friends, relatives and even
oneself, but the Power within is not deceived.
Saint Sawan Singh, 20th Century

For he who is honest is noble,
whatever his fortunes or birth.
Alice Cary
Nobility

Try not to become a man of success
but rather to become a man of value.
Dr. Albert Einstein

An honest man's the noblest work of God.
Alexander Pope

If we are to live with a noble and elevated spirit, regardless of our personal comfort, it is axiomatic that we realize that *Character Must Precede Prowess.* In other words, character must come first before our martial arts rank, status, championships, name, fame, skill, billfold, bank account, titles on the door, trophies on the shelf, name plates on the desk, headlines in the local society column or records in the record book. Without a high ethical and moral character, of what true value is our life? Regardless of our achievements, if we lack a sound character, how can we be truly satisfied with ourselves as human beings and the legacy we will leave upon the earth when our last breath is expended?

Yet, how often is the great ideal of personal character sacrificed for the passing pleasures, ephemeral accomplishments and empty titles of this world? Who is there, what is there that extols the nobility of personal character? Where are the virtue schools in our society? Where are the headlines praising those whose lives are wrapped with the garments of virtue? For the most part, those who are lauded, applauded and praised in a daze are saturated with energies far from that which speaks to a noble character.

Thankfully, there are higher powers that recognize and reward higher values and virtues. As martial artists, as those individuals on a path of self-improvement and personal integration, we should be one part of society that teaches and expresses that which is noble, good, decent, kind, caring, compassionate and magnanimous. If not us, then who?

#10

A Black Belt
Without Humility Is Like
A Well Without Water

Humility is the highest form of strength;

Arrogance the highest form of weakness.

As a silo sits vacant of fodder,

A Black Belt Without Humility

Is Like A Well Without Water.

We come nearest to the great

when we are great in humility.

Rabindranath Tagore

[Nobel Laureate, Literature 1913]

To become truly great, one has to

stand with people, not above them.

Charles de Montesquieu

[18th Century French Philosopher]

If I have seen further, it is only by

standing on the shoulders of Giants.

Sir Isaac Newton

There is absolutely no question that the greatest of souls to ever walk and breathe upon the earth were saturated from head to toe and bone to soul with humility. Of all the virtues, none stands equal to a genuine heart fully replete with its own insignificance. Indisputably, the greatest of the great clothe and cloak themselves in the garb of honest humility. They intrinsically understand their connection to an infinite power far greater than the finite scope of their limited selves, as well as their duty to be a conduit of compassion for all.

Martial arts is a great magnet for the power-driven consciousness. Because of its capacity to create warriors of extreme skill and combative prowess, it often, and most unfortunately, attracts the ego-saturated and machismo-laden intimidator who, in a quest to manage his intrinsic insecurity, over-compensates by bullying externally, pronouncing himself in the manner of a chest-thumping gorilla or a feather-strutting peacock. Such behavior is not power. It is unadulterated weakness masquerading as power. Hopefully, through the rigors and discipline of martial arts training, such souls will gain the inner strength they need to overcome their weakness, become truly strong, and walk the path of those who wear the mantle of magnanimity, not malevolence or vulgarity.

Because martial arts creates power - not just in martial combat but in character, it is practically incumbent on the practitioner to be humble, realizing the importance of the mystic phrase from Saint Charan Singh: *Only the highest can help the lowest.* Of what value is there anyway in lauding oneself over another? It is, to be sure, a clear sign of insecurity prima facia [on its face]. The reality of power is that it *is* powerful and needs no advertisement. The famous British Prime Minister, Margaret Thatcher, said: *Being powerful is like being a lady. If you have to tell people you are, you aren't.* So why would any Black Belt worth his rank need to conduct himself or herself in such a way as to promote their own prowess? Their prowess should be a reflection of their humility, not their machismo. Look at the truly great souls who have walked this planet: Buddha, Christ, Kabir, Guru Nanak, Schweitzer, Mother Teresa, Gandhi and others. Their power was reflected in their humility, not their arrogance. As martial artists, it is appropriate, if not dutiful, that we demonstrate the reality that *A Black Belt Without Humility is Like a Well Without Water.*

#11

True Power Flows
Not Shows

From dusk to dawn the world goes

circling sun with highs and lows;

within this journey Greatness knows

True Power Flows Not Shows.

Learn this from the waters:

in mountain clefts and chasms

loud gush the streamlets,

but great rivers run silently.

Things that are empty make a noise;

the full is always quiet.

Buddha

This is a very simple truth which needs no great explanation. If we are truly powerful, our power will flow from us as easily as water down a mountain. It will not be forced. It need not be announced. It will just flow and it will flow silently as great rivers flow silently.

It's is sure bet that those who make a great effort to be powerful, to be dominant, to be imposing are simply trying to express externally what they lack internally - a healthy, whole and integrated sense of self. To repeat Margaret Thatcher's statement: *Being powerful is like being a lady. If you have to tell people you are, you aren't.* Likewise, in being a Black Belt if we have to tell people we are powerful to substantiate our confidence, or make some external show or create some "noise" to validate our achievement, we would be well-served to evaluate our substantive sense of self. In other words, true power should flow from a Black Belt naturally with neither declaration or exhibition. So should it be for all intrinsically powerful people. If they are truly powerful, their power will flow from them easily, effortlessly, quietly.

On a personal note, in my competitive days, the fighters that gave me pause and coalesced my attention to action were not the ones with the loud mouths and ostentatious displays of power, but those who were relaxed, calm, composed, quiet, confident and self-assured. They needed no show. They knew who they were and what their skills were. They were true warriors. Their power was genuine and they knew it. Subsequently, their power flowed . . . silently, and never showed until the moment of truth when the battle engaged.

#12

Competence Creates Confidence

Action and reaction;

Cause and consequence.

It is no mystery that

Competence Creates Confidence.

Reason's whole pleasure,

all the joys of sense,

Lie in three words, -

health, peace, and competence.

Alexander Pope

[Essay on Man]

Nothing creates confidence more than competence. Telling someone they're good at something, giving them pats on the back, kisses on the cheek, big hugs and positive words of how great they are don't, nor can't, build true confidence. Only competence creates confidence.

Suppose a martial arts instructor, instead of teaching his students the skills, techniques and mindset of self-defense, simply tells his students they are good, gives them mantras to repeat, concepts to think about, a kind word, a pat on the back, a diploma of rank stating they are this or that belt designation, and then a smile of good will as they leave the studio. What can this possibly do to create any semblance of confidence? Not only does it do nothing to help insure the individual's self-defense capability, it does great harm because the student may potentially acquire a false sense of his abilities which could easily get him injured or worse. The name of the game for any competent martial arts instructor is to create competence in his students. This is done by giving them skills first and kudos second if they're deserved. Skills before kudos. This should be the mantric basis of the principle *competence creates confidence*. When we give kudos before skills, we weaken the individual and potentially disable him from defending his life if need be.

True story. One aspect of women's self-defense training at the Karate Institute of America is, when in public, to always be aware of "who's watching you?" In simple terms, be aware of your environment and don't assume a Pollyanna approach to life by being overly and illogically optimistic or being an ostrich with its head buried in the sand, thinking that if you can't see danger, it won't affect you. The Pollyanna-Ostrich syndrome is a recipe for disaster. Look around. Take note of where you are. Don't assume you're not being watched, surveilled or targeted and that you need no defenses. The sad truth of this world is that we must always be aware and prepared to defend ourselves or our loved ones if need be. This is not paradise. It would be a mistake to believe it is.

As destiny would have it, two weeks after this particular workshop, one of the ladies was in a grocery store. Having been schooled in the principle, "Who's watching you?", she noticed a man kept watching and following her wherever she went. She'd go down an isle, he would follow. She'd go down another isle, he'd follow suit. When she went to the checkout counter, so did he. When she exited the store, got in her car and drove away, he followed in his car. Noticing she was being stalked, she drove right to the nearest police station and her would-be assailant drove on, never to be seen again.

What saved this woman was her awareness, her competence in managing her life on a daily basis. Her training protected her, as all training is designed to do. It was this competence that gave her the confidence to handle the situation. By her own admission, before the workshop she went about her day without an awareness of her environment. What could have happened had she not been aware of her surroundings and watching out for who was possibly watching her? Thank God she'll never know, and kudos to her for taking a few hours to invest in not just her well-being, but her life.

The bottom line in all this is that when we have skill, we have confidence. We don't acquire confidence by being skillless. In whatever we do in life, if we want confidence and the joy and peace that come with it, we must expend the time, effort and possibly money to create the competence insuring that confidence, which in turn, as in the case of this woman, could well save our life.

#13

Substance
Before
Symbol

Symbol before substance -

pandemic renowned.

Symbol before substance -

deluded clown.

Substance Before Symbol -

turn it around.

Substance Before Symbol -

deservéd crown!

Beware that you do not lose the substance
by grasping at the shadow.
Aesop

Be not deceived with the first appearance of things,
for show is not substance.
English proverb

The leader shows that style is
no substitute for substance.
Lao Tzu

In so many ways the civilization of the 21st Century lives in the delusion that symbol is more important than substance, that the character of who we are has been turned inside-out and upside-down to where it's more important to be superficially adorned with the trappings of celebrity, fame, name, power, wealth, status, popularity and gamesmanship than it is to be anchored in principles of character, humility, honesty, honor, dignity, purity and substance.

When we sacrifice substance for symbol, we destroy the nobility inherent in our spirit and play the role of clown while foregoing the crown of all that is decent, whole and noble. For example, this is an age where black belt rankings are quite often placed on the sale block and sold for thirty pieces of silver, or less, by unscrupulous individuals who care nothing for their character or reputations, let alone those of the art. Their focus is centered in the size of their bank accounts rather than in the size of their student's progress, achievement and well-being. This kind of behavior not only dilutes the great meaning of martial arts training, but it also casts a dark cloud over it, diminishing the art as a whole, negatively impacting future generations.

Three true stories. The first involves an individual who wanted a black belt rating so he could show it on his resume and get a promotion from the organization that employed him which wanted to see extracurricular activities on his resume. Rather than expend the effort and time to obtain a competent black belt rating from a reputable studio, he enrolled in a school which promised him a black belt for a specific price within a year. He paid his money, got his "black belt" and probably his promotion. Black Belt in a year? For a certain amount of money? Can excellence be purchased? Can attainment be promised within a time limit? Can a piano enthusiast become a concert pianist or competent performer in a year? Unlikely. Same for becoming a true Black Belt. A legitimate black belt program involves years of study, five at the least, if the curriculum is worthy and varied, one teaching basic skills, fighting, kata [forms], weapons, self-defense techniques and extemporaneous combat. Attaining a so-called black belt in today's world has become so watered down it is shameful, not to mention dangerous. If a person is a Black Belt, he or she had better be a Black Belt in the truest sense of the word. Not only are the courts going to hold such a person accountable for his actions should the event ever arise, but the individual's life, and possibly the lives and well-being of others, could be at stake.

Second story. A gentleman had been in a rush to get a black belt rating because it holds a certain degree of respect which he felt would give him respect in the eyes of others. After attaining a purple belt [an advanced beginner status], he visited a competitive studio in which the instructor invited him into his office and asked him to demonstrate six ways to kill a human being. Having been in the military, the man demonstrated six ways of taking someone's life, whereupon the instructor awarded him a black belt on the spot and entered him into their organization's log as a black belt!

Third story. This is just as ludicrous as the second, but true nonetheless. An organization, separate from the previous one, advertised a one-day black belt training and promotion workshop. For a price of $150, participants would receive training on a

Saturday from 9:00am to 11:30am, break for lunch, resume training from 1:00 pm to 3:30pm, and then be awarded a black belt at the end of the event! The ad promised that the individual would also be certified by the hosting martial arts organization. Is this the great height to which our culture has aspired, instant black belt?

The reality is that none of the individuals who granted or received a so-called black belt rating in these stories was competent, let alone ethical. Yet, this kind of instant gratification, make-it-easy-for-me behavior has been instrumental in devaluing the rich legacy of black belt legitimacy. Any accomplishment of merit takes time and effort. Nothing of any true worth, especially that of attaining a black belt, is accomplished without hard work, dedication, devotion, determination, patience, persistence and courage for an extended period of time. Competence creates confidence as noted earlier. Regardless of the subject involved, especially that of a performing art, excellence involves sweat and tears for years in order to achieve a level of expertise.

In the world of martial arts, the Black Belt is a symbol of excellence awarded and rewarded *after* the student develops the *substance* to support it. This would seem to be common sense, and it is. Yet, there are those who think differently. For them, it's all about the symbol, not the substance. For those in pursuit of a true black belt, here is some instructor advice: as long as you hold to the *substance before symbol* principle, you will be able to walk with dignity and nobility in life. However, make sure you are worthy of the black belt before you put it on because you will be known for what you are or, more tragically, for what you are not.

#14
The Road To Success Is Paved With Failure

Within the heart emotions stir.

Failure is not what we prefer;

but yet, the victors all confer -

The Road To Success Is Paved With Failure.

Success consists of going from failure to failure
without loss of enthusiasm.

Success is not final, failure is not fatal:
it is the courage to continue that counts.
Sir Winston Churchill

Most people give up just when they're about to
achieve success. They quit on the one yard line.
They give up at the last minute of the game,
one foot from a winning touchdown.
Ross Perot

We live in a dual dimension. There is positive; there is negative. There is day; there is night. There is high; there is low; masculine and feminine; hard and soft; hot and cold; on and off; up and down, war and peace and . . . success and failure.

All of the components of these pairs share opposite sides of the same energetic coin. We can't have one and escape the other. It's impossible. When we hold a coin in our hand, we hold both sides simultaneously. The key to managing opposites is to find the Golden Mean or balance point between the two sides and not to become imbalanced by focusing on one side to the exclusion of the other. The other is there, and as long as we're aware of it and work with it we can lead a meaningful and fulfilling life.

In the case of success and failure, each is part of the other as reflected in the Yin/Yang symbol of the Chinese Tao. In this ancient pictorial motif there exists a black dot in the white hemisphere and a white dot in the black hemisphere representing the truth of intrinsically connected opposites. Failure does not stand alone. Nor does success. They are two halves of the same whole.

Unfortunately, this concept is overlooked or not understood. Too often, failure is feared, subsequently fatally wounding the aspirant in search of success. In other words, some people quit because they think failure is something bad or to be ashamed of when in reality it is an integral part of the success process. To succeed, we have to expect failure so we can learn from our mistakes and ultimately succeed. It's just a process, and through it we come to the unambiguous and incontrovertible conclusion that *the road to success is paved with failure.*

So whose failure is the road to success paved with? It's paved with the failure of others and our own, mostly our own. In studying the lives of people who have failed and ultimately succeeded, by their experiences we learn what to do and what not to do. Their journeys can help us lay the pavestones for our own roads to success.

Abraham Lincoln was, arguably, the greatest president in United States history. The power, strength, wisdom and savvy this great soul expressed are immense. Read a little about his life. It is a beautiful example of how *the road to success is paved with failure,* each failure honing his spirit, creating more wisdom, making him stronger, giving him more resolve, more desire, more knowledge to build a legacy of failure and success that would be hard to match. Did he set out fail? Of course not. No one sets out to fail, but we all do. Lincoln certainly did. He failed . . . and failed . . . and failed and kept failing. He failed so much before he became the tremendously successful giant he was that in reading his life story one has to plead to God to give him a break. Yet, thank God that He didn't give Lincoln a break. It was Lincoln's failures that created a legacy of greatness of extreme worthiness and helped create the United States of America, a country that was not united and found itself in the middle of a great and tragic civil war in which brothers were killing brothers. It was a horrible time in American history, but if not for the strength, courage, wisdom, resolve and tenacity of Abraham Lincoln, it might never have become united. Thank God for failures!

The Black Belt Book of Life   King

The more substantive failures from which we learn, however, are our own. Why? Because we feel them more, often painfully, and when things hurt on a personal level, we're far more apt to take action and correct the mistakes than if the failures were someone else's.

True story. This one addresses *the greatest fight I ever lost*, a fight whose failures had enormous positive impact on the fighting curriculum of the Karate Institute of America and the Kiado-Ryu system of marital arts, a fight whose outcome is so vivid I can clearly remember it to this day, decades after the event. It is also a fight I thank God I lost, not won, and which underscores the fact that *the road to success is paved with failure.*

The fight took place at a karate tournament in the mid 1980s. In preparation for the tournament, I had been working on new movement theories which incorporated an array of directional and angular changes, jukes, stutters, rollouts and motion nuances. As the fight began, I began applying these new theories. I was scoring on my opponent well and often, or so I thought. When I would score a point in my mind, the head official would deny it. He did this time and time again. I became frustrated. I calculated the final score to be six to two in my favor. A post review of the video by a highly respected black belt confirmed the fight should have ended in a six/two win for me. But in reality, and because of the subjective nature of competitive martial arts point fighting in those days, I ended up losing the fight three to two, and am I glad I did!

From an official standpoint, the fight was tied two to two with seconds left on the clock. I was circling my opponent in a counter clockwise direction when Bam!, I got clocked with a left backfist to my face, thus giving my opponent an ultimate three to two win. Of course in the moment I was upset until the final judgment was delivered by the referee at the center of the ring. When he announced my opponent as the winner, my opponent exploded in a screaming vertical leap, landing in a low squat position, pounding his chest with his fists . . . still screaming . . . and exulting in his victory. In was an awesome display of emotion. Although I had officially lost the fight, all I could do was contain my own joy, laughter and composure because my opponent was, by his overt and hyperbolic enthusiasm, telling me that the movement theories I was applying were working! He had become so frustrated in trying to hit me and not being able to do so during the contest as much as he would have liked, that after the fight his emotions got the better of him. He was ecstatic outwardly; I was ecstatic inwardly. Had this man not been so externally demonstrative, I never would have known that the movement theories I had been employing and working diligently to create and improve were working! To this day I am grateful for not only having lost that fight but for this man telegraphing his emotions. His actions confirmed the theories of fighting movement I had been developing, thus encouraging me to keep developing them.

Losing this fight was a great failure. Had I succeeded, I never would have had a clue that what I was doing was working. I would have simply basked in the ephemeral limelight and glory of the moment, patted myself on the back and gone on, not the wiser for what really happened.

There was more to that contest that underscored why it was *the greatest fight I ever lost.* Besides cementing the movement theories, when he hit me with that backfist in the final seconds to officially win the match - and it was a good shot, it taught me that my guard was ineffective and weak, causing me to reconstruct it in such a way that a newly designed guard structure was practically impenetrable. Had I not taken that shot to my face, I never would have developed the more efficient and protective guard that resulted in many victories. This was a great second boon to having failed.

From this second failure, a new cardinal fighting sin emerged: "Never get hit with a backfist." To be hit and scored upon with this weapon meant one of two things: 1. the guard was weak and incorrectly structured, which we've discussed, and 2. I was too close to my opponent. Had I kept my distance, he wouldn't have been able to score on me. This later realization caused me to readjust my understanding of fighting distance.

These *failures* resulted in dynamic changes to our Kiado-Ryu fighting curriculum which is superior to that which it had been but which would never have come into existence had I succeeded in winning that particular fight. It was a great moment, but it was a moment that most people would regard as one of *failure*, not success. The irony, of course, is that it was a great success because it ignited a whole new restructuring of Kiado-Ryu fighting theory. It was, indeed, a perfect example of how *the road to success is paved with failure.*

The moral of the story: don't be afraid to fail! Learn from your mistakes, be grateful for them and move on, allowing your own failures to pave the way to your successes.

#15
Strength Is The Ability
To Endure

The meanings of strength are many,

but one thing is for sure,

in the struggle-strewn strife of life

Strength Is The Ability To Endure.

You only have to endure to conquer.

Winston Churchill

What does not kill me makes me stronger.

Goethe

The strongest man in the world

is he who stands most alone.

Henrik Ibsen

Strength does not come from physical capacity.

It comes from an indomitable will.

Gandhi

Being deeply loved by someone gives you strength,

while loving someone deeply gives you courage.

Lao Tzu

L ife is a test from birth to death; an endless struggle to maintain one's balance, poise and grace while striving to achieve one's personal goals. If we're to conquer the challenges of life, we must be strong . . . for the long haul, not just for the passing moment or the fleeting glimpses of capricious fortune.

Strength is a virtue. Talent is a gift. One can have talent but fail to achieve great things because of a lack of strength. One can have mediocre talent but achieve wondrous things through the strength of will.

As an example, in the history of the Karate Institute of America, there have been some very noteworthy physically talented individuals who never succeeded in becoming a Black Belt because they lacked the strength [the ability to endure] to achieve the goal, some giving up the ghost just weeks before their final exam. Contrastingly, there have been many individuals who, lacking great talent, succeeded in achieving a Black Belt rating because they never quit. They fought, struggled, endured and saw the journey through to its conclusion. In fact, if there is one quality of all Kiado-Ryu Black Belts, it is that they all expressed an indomitable will and relentless spirit to succeed. Their strength exceeded the challenges and adversities they faced in their martial arts journey. Such is the truth in every discipline, in every line of work. Those who succeed never quit.

At the Karate Institute of America there is a tradition of honoring each individual who achieved the rank of Black Belt by hanging a black belt embroidered with their name and coronation date on the walls of the studio. In effect, this becomes a visual living testimony to their accomplishments in the same fashion that collegiate and professional sports institutions honor their champions with banners on their walls, ceilings and facades. The following two poems, entitled *The Wall* and *The Wall II*, are included on the following two pages as another means of honoring their accomplishments of strength and character.

THE WALL

It stands, unyielding, to an ever-present flow of suppliants:
THE WALL

It beckons, calling and challenging those
whose spirit would be tested in the fire:
THE WALL

It rewards and holds within its bosom and on its face
those individuals who came to challenge and to conquer
and prove their spirit equal to the task:
THE WALL

It honors and presents forever to the world
those collective souls whose spirits would never die,
would never yield to the fire of its own relentless spirit:
THE WALL

It stands as a grand and noble legacy for grand and
noble conquerors - Black Belts of the Kiado-Ryu.
It is their exclusive right, their exclusive heritage,
their exclusive destiny.
It is undeniably and unquestionably
their WALL.

The Black Belt Book of Life   King

THE WALL II

They have come in multitudes, for decades.

Through their sweat, blood, tears,

hopes and dreams they have come --

Seeking, striving to reach a pinnacle

only few have conquered;

Seeking to rise above

the mediocre and mundane

to stand apart in triumph!

But the Wall, standing as an edifice

to courage, determination and the

substance of a relentless spirit,

has broken all but just a few --

The few who could not be broken;

The few who would not be broken;

The few who can truly claim to be named

Black Belts of the Kiado-Ryu!

We all have challenges in life, tests which demand our strength, our ability to endure adversities, reversals, heartbreaks, heartaches, setbacks and temporary failures. If we're to ultimately succeed, however, we must exercise an indomitable will. In the game of life, talent is a good thing to have, but strength - the ability to endure to the end, is indispensible.

#16

Not To But Through

In finding the mark and hitting it,

as we our goals pursue,

the key to raising the Cup is

Not To But Through.

I can give you a six-word formula for success:
Think things through - then follow through.
Sir Walter Scott

In martial arts, one of the keys to generating devastating power is penetrating the target, i.e., not focusing *to* the target but rather *through* the target. When we strike at the front of a target, even though we may hit it, our strike will have little effect because of its lack of depth. However, if rather than merely hitting the target, we project and strike *through* it, our effective power will be greatly enhanced.

As an example, if you are a martial artist, next time you do some bag work, focus your punches six to twelve inches beyond the target. Given the same speed, trajectory and technique of the punch, the power output will be greater. Follow the same principle

The Black Belt Book of Life   King

of all strikes and kicks. Focus *not to* the target *but through* the target for maximum effect.

To illustrate the potency of this principle, practice the following *Focus, Nick* and *Stick* drill. From your position in front of a bag, dummy or makiwara board, deliver a punch full power and *focus* it an inch in front of the target without hitting it. Do five reps. Then adjust your punch to only *nick* the target. Use the same amount of energy in delivering the punch. Do this for five reps. Then, adjust your concentration six to twelve inches beyond the front of the target and punch *through* it with the same intensity used for the two previous punches, the *focus* and the *nick*. Do this also for five reps. See the difference of focusing *through* the target and with the same amount of energy expenditure? It's much greater. As a follow-up drill, execute the *Focus, Nick* and *Stick* drill in succession, one punch following the other. This will help develop control. A good Black Belt should be able to focus, nick or stick his target at will with total control with any of his weapons, whether those weapons are punches, kicks, backfists, elbows, knees, armbars, palms, chops or ridgehands.

Although the previous example uses a martial arts exercise, the same principle applies to any problem in life. When we focus not *to* the target but *through* it, not only will we have greater power but we'll also have greater consistency in the results.

Another example. Ever watch a sprinter in a track and field race start slowing down *before* he crosses the finish line? It's a common problem. Why do this? To achieve the best time possible and insure a victory, the key is to run full speed *through* the finish line, not to it. Furthermore, it's an excellent rule in life to always focus *through* and *go through* the problem to develop the habit of always finishing strongly. If we don't practice mentally, physically and spiritually moving through the target [the goal at hand], we'll potentially fall short. To insure success in anything we do, it is important to focus *not to but through* the task at hand.

How does this apply to life? If you need to save $100, focus on saving $200. If you want to get an A in a class, think of getting an A+ or doing extra credit to insure an A. If you need to make five sales calls in a given time period, focus on ten. If you want to lose twenty pounds, focus on thirty. If you're writing a book, rather than setting a goal of writing three pages a day, write five. You've got the picture. Always focus beyond and *through* the target for maximum results.

Regarding the journey of life itself, if we are to make the most of our life, it would be wise to focus beyond the grave to the next life, to the next phase of our journey. This life is only one part of our existence. There will be other parts, other phases. By focusing on our death in this life and considering our death to be the end, we limit the success of not only this life but our next life. The admonition is, *not to but through*. Therefore, to make the most of this life and prepare for the next, we need to focus *beyond* the grave to the next phase. This strategy will insure that our energetic *link of life* is not broken, thus solidifying the continuity of our existence and our soul's ultimate triumph.

#17

Preparation Is The Key To Success

With any project you undertake,

to limit stress and insure progress,

the cardinal rule is simply this:

Preparation Is The Key To Success.

To be prepared is half the victory.

Miguel De Cervantes

[Author of *Don Quixote*]

Luck favors the mind that is prepared.

Louis Pasteur

Before everything else,

getting ready is the secret to success.

Henry Ford

If I had eight hours to chop down a tree,

I'd spend six hours sharpening my ax.

Abraham Lincoln

The Black Belt Book of Life   King

If you fail to prepare, you prepare to fail. This maxim underscores the importance of preparation in any undertaking or project. If we're going to slay some dragons, we'd better spend a great deal of time creating a plan, rehearsing it and sharpening the blade of our axe or sword *before* the battle is engaged.

Lincoln's statement offers a good model in establishing the amount of time devoted to a project's preparation and its actual execution. He says if he had eight hours to chop down a tree, he'd spend six hours sharpening his ax. Six hours is three quarters or 75% of the entire time devoted to the project! That's enormous. Yet, if one were to query the most successful individuals in any field, the results would most likely be very similar.

There's another maxim which adds texture and meaning to the preparation concept. It's this: *if you don't do it right the first time, how much time will it take to do it right the second time?* And then how much time, money, energy, effort, man-power will be lost in having to get it right, not to mention the dilemma of having to then overcome the depression, frustration, anxiety and let-down of having to do it all over again. Do-overs may be necessary but they can be potentially avoided if one were to functionally understand that *Preparation is the Key to Success.* The moral of the maxim: prepare, prepare, prepare or despair, despair, despair!

#18

There Can Be No
Excellence Without
Effort

We live in an age with effort waning,

with riches expected sans work;

but in all reality and actuality

There Can Be No Excellence Without Effort.

Much effort, much prosperity.

Euripides

Success is dependent on effort.

Sophocles

The mode by which the inevitable comes to pass is effort.

Oliver Wendell Holmes

I'm a great believer in luck, and I find
the harder I work the more I have of it.

Thomas Jefferson

It is only through labor and painful effort, by grim energy and
resolute courage, that we move on to better things.

Theodore Roosevelt

T here's just no way around it. Excellence and success take work. People may try to find short cuts, even sacrifice their ethics and morality to acquire it, but in the end the age old truth relating effort to success holds true: *There can be no excellence without effort.*

Unfortunately, the martial arts world has been the target of some individuals who have preyed on the instant-gratification yearnings of those who want a shortcut to being a Black Belt. Without any knowledge to the contrary, and caught up in their own desires, these souls get duped into believing the achievement of a Black Belt can be attained in a short amount of time with a certain amount of money.

Of course the martial arts industry claims no exclusivity of such behavior. Trying to find a short cut to excellence is prevalent in our society and has even reared its head in the most honorable of institutions which have registered cheating scandals: the U.S. Naval Academy at Annapolis, the U.S. Military Academy at West Point, and the U.S. Air Force Academy at Colorado Springs.

Unfortunately, in the human race there will always be those who try to find a short cut to excellence, trading their dignity, nobility, character, reputation and future in the process. Some may succeed for a while, even a season, but in the end the truth will always be revealed. In the world of excellence, there are simply no short cuts. To be good at anything requires substantive dedication and work because, simply, *there can be no excellence without effort.*

#19
Rank Does Not Make The Man. The Man Makes The Rank

In a world of slippery, empty titles,

this truth to God we thank:

Rank Does Not Make The Man,

The Man Makes The Rank.

Ranks of this world will not

be recognized in the next.

Guru Nanak

[15th/16th Century Saint]

High rank and soft manners may not

always belong to a true heart.

Anthony Trollope

[19th Century English novelist]

It is an interesting question how far men

would retain their relative rank if they

were divested of their clothes.

Henry David Thoreau

The achievement of a black belt from a reputable martial arts establishment is a rank of notable merit, as any Black Belt will confirm. It takes an enormous amount of sacrifice, dedication, determination, persistence, effort, time, sweat, pain and focus to achieve. Yet, as any dedicated Black Belt will also tell you, such a prestigious rank does not make him who he is. It is he who makes the rank what it is, and thus, *rank does not make the man; the man makes the rank.*

This philosophy applies to any worthy position in any field of endeavor. Does donning a black belt or acquiring a designation of any sort make a person wiser, more loving, kind, aware, gifted or better than another person? If God created us all, how could any one person consider himself better than another? Spiritually speaking, he can't. Titles do not make men. Men make titles. Ranks do not make men. Men make ranks.

Yet, in this world a person's station in life somehow places him in a certain class category with the rich and famous at the top and the poor and infamous at the bottom. Titles often expand people's egos, giving them a false sense of superiority. As the famous 18th Century French writer, Suzanne Necker, observed: *Fortune does not change men, it unmasks them.* Equating title, rank or position to superiority is an illusion. Think of the greatest souls in history. The quality that made them great above all others was not their station in life but their humility. Lao Tzu, Buddha, Christ, Guru Nanak, Kabir, Ravidas, Gandhi, Schweitzer, Mother Teresa and others became great not because of their titles but because of who they were, not what they were.

The Black Belt Book of Life   King

As we achieve, whether in the martial arts world, the sports world, corporate world, educational world, medical world, media world, etc., if we're to become truly worthy of any rank, we need to give worthiness to that rank, not allow it to give worthiness to us, to control us, or increase the ego that is us. If we assume a sense of entitlement and superiority because of our rank or title, we fail in the test of power. In fact, the higher we go, the greater our responsibility to not violate the spiritual principles of power or humility. What God gives He can certainly take away, and those in power would do well to heed this advice. As Guru Nanak states, *Ranks of this world will not be recognized in the next.* Therefore, those who have been bequeathed great power and position now, in this lifetime, should pause and look beyond the gates of death lest any misuse of their ephemeral status in the "here and now" places them, not on pedestals, but on pin cushions in the "there and then."

Great minds throughout history have warned about the abuse of power. Following are some worthy quotes for consideration.

Uneasy lies the head that wears a crown.
> ~ Shakespeare: Henry IV, Part 2, Act 3, Scene 1

Power tends to corrupt, and absolute power corrupts absolutely. Great men are almost always bad men.
> ~ Lord Acton

No man is wise enough, nor good enough to be trusted with unlimited power.
> ~ Charles Caleb Colton

Power, like a desolating pestilence, pollutes whatever it touches.

~ Percy Shelley

The boast of heraldry, the pomp of power, and all that beauty, all that wealth e're gave, awaits alike the inevitable hour. The paths of glory lead but to the grave.

~ Thomas Gray
Elegy Written in a Country Church-yard

Unnumbered suppliants crowd Preferment's Gate, athirst for wealth and burning to be great; delusive fortune hears the incessant call; they rise, they shine, evaporate and fall!

~ Dr. Samuel Johnson
Vanity of Human Wishes

All is ephemeral,—fame and the famous as well.

~ Marcus Aurelius 2nd Century AD

The moral of this section: when given rank or status, treat it as if you were walking on eggs, the razor's edge or on a precipice. Know it is temporary and not to be lauded over others. If anything, having status is a call to service, not rulership. As the great Dr. Albert Einstein stated: *The highest destiny of the individual is to serve rather than to rule.*

#20
Control Is The Mark
Of A Master

In quest to master any art
and avoid unkind disaster,
it would be wise to recognize
Control Is The Mark Of A Master.

Only one who devotes himself to a cause
with his whole strength and soul can be
a true master. For this reason mastery
demands all of a person.
Albert Einstein

The happiness of a man in this life does
not consist in the absence but in
the mastery of his passions.
Alfred Lord Tennyson

All of your scholarship, all your study of Shakespeare
and Wordsworth would be vain if at the same time you
did not build your character and attain mastery
over your thoughts and your actions.
Gandhi

T he ultimate goal of devoting oneself to any discipline is to master that discipline. To master it is to control it. Because of its dangerous and potentially lethal aspects, martial arts is one discipline that must instill mastery in its practitioners.

Martial arts mastery exists on multiple levels. First, there is the obvious skill of learning to master the strikes, blocks, parries, kicks, punches, moves, self-defense and fighting techniques, as well as open hand and weapons forms. Intrinsically tied to this is the control of one's balance, especially under stress. Then there is the great task of learning to control one's emotions and mental abilities. No other discipline teaches one to integrate his body, mind and spirit more than the martial arts. In essence, martial arts teaches one to master himself.

As all things in this dimension have two sides, mastery of one's self also has two sides: external and internal. *External mastery* involves the skills intrinsic to the martial arts system the individual is studying, as referenced above. *Internal mastery* focuses on slaying our inner dragons and fears. Unless we reveal these to others, they are secret and known only to us. For example, we may have challenges with our identity, image, courage, fear, discipline, persistence, unworthiness, weakness, self-confidence, strength, procrastination, follow-through, emotional stability and many other issues. Slaying the dragon or dragons within us is a great aspect of martial arts training. It is impossible to participate in a worthy program and not have any or all of one's demons rearing their heads and engaging us in personal combat. Our task is to challenge them head on, take them on and slay them. In doing so we develop a great sense of personal accomplishment and centeredness that only we can know and appreciate. After all, these are our battles, as well they should be. No one else has to know about them except us.

External mastery not only involves the artistic and physical things alluded to earlier but also to other people and situations - the external dragons. For example, let's say some social crisis occurs. 911 comes to mind. How do we respond? Do we "lose it and fall apart?" Do we freeze in place and become immobilized through fear or just not knowing what to do? Or do we remain centered, calm and balanced, think clearly and take appropriate action?

Then there is the issue of other people preying on us? If we're being assaulted, how do we respond? Give up and possibly die? Hope our assailant doesn't hurt us? Do we try to appease the perpetrator, remembering the wisdom of Winston Churchill who said: *An appeaser is one who feeds a crocodile hoping it will eat him last?* Or do we protect ourselves with the best and wisest choice appropriate to the environment, situation and surroundings? This may involve simply speaking to our assailant to back him down, fleeing the scene perhaps, or engaging him physically. This last option requires sagacious and often quick thought and action. In effect, what action do we take to master the situation given all the variables involved?

True story. This is common to us all and comes under the heading of "response to the finger." You know what I mean. One day I was in my car stopped at a red light minding my own business. An oncoming car was making a left hand turn on his green arrow and as the car turned into his lane, thus becoming perpendicular to the forward direction of my car but some thirty feet away, for whatever reason this young teenage guy in the passenger seat put his arm out the window and flipped me the finger as he scowled and attempted to look somewhat frightful. It was pretty funny actually because this event came out of nowhere and was totally unexpected. In applying techniques of mastery, I didn't react in a negative capacity but rather returned his gesture with a big smile and a wave of my hand, certainly not my finger. His reaction was typical of this sort of misanthrope. He went absolutely ballistic, becoming even more enraged and red than he was in the first place as the car continued on.

In analyzing this scenario, what would have happened if I had returned a finger to him and shouted some unbecoming remark as he went on his way? Nothing likely because this sort of thing happens all the time, especially with young men stuffed to the brim and overflowing with testosterone and foolishness. But the key is that if I had responded in a negative way, I would have moved outside my own center, engaged in an immature and ignoble act while relinquishing control of myself to this kid, an act that could have potentially escalated into something worse. In behaving in such a manner, I would have been nothing more than a dog on his leash - he the controller [the master] and I the controlee [the dog], which is probably what he was expecting, as most people who engage in this sort of conduct do expect. They like to control the situation in whatever way they can. By reacting in a totally different manner - waving politely with a smile on my face, it totally disarmed this kid and collapsed his guard. I was now in control - of myself and the situation. He wasn't, and he didn't know what to do but get madder and hotter and flip his finger more exuberantly.

This whole scenario is an example of exhibiting skills of mastery which we teach at the Karate Institute of America. Behaving in such a controlled way to an external act places us in the driver's seat, keeps us calm and in control of the situation. Others have also used this with equal success, and for the younger generation it is highly recommended because it removes us from a position of being controlled, and therefore being out of control, to being totally in control and not allowing the situation to get out of hand. Another option to having the "finger" flashed at you is to simply ignore it altogether and do nothing. The non-smart thing to do is to respond in kind by flipping your finger back at the perpetrator. That's exactly what he wants. Don't play his game. Make sure you play your game and take him out of his. In this way, you'll be the one holding the leash and he'll be the one on it, i.e., you'll be the master and he'll be the whimpering puppy.

Remember Pythagoras? He was the ancient mathematician and philosopher who said, *No man is free who cannot control himself.* This coincides with Tennyson who advised us to control our passions and Gandhi who adjured us to control our thoughts and actions. Their quotes are placed in the opening to this section. All great teachers preach the necessity of self-control and ultimately of self-mastery.

Martial arts is an excellent discipline to meet these ends. As practitioners, it would be good for us to remember that *the process*

84

is the product. The Black Belt, should we evolve to its level, is a symbol of the *process*, a process that is invaluable to not only our self-protection and well-being in a physical sense, but also to our growth as individuals.

As was stated early on in this book, *martial arts is life.* There is nothing we do in our training that does not have some functional life application beyond the studio/dojo/gym doors, and if all we're concerned with in our training is learning how to beat someone up or defend ourselves physically, we've missed a great opportunity and gift. Remember the phrase, *a black belt without humility is like a well without water?* Well, if we go to the well of martial arts and return with only knowledge related to physical defense and combat, it's like going to the well with an empty bucket and returning with nothing more than a mere spoonful of water. Such an act is a great disservice to what martial arts study and training bequeaths to us who love it so. And at its core, arguably the greatest gift of martial arts training is the gift of self-control and self-mastery because to be sure, *control is the mark of a master.*

#21
Diamond Casting

Diamonds are made under extreme heat and pressure

over an extended period of time, not

by a mere and casual blowing

of an intermittent wind.

We could never learn to be brave and patient
if there were only joy in the world.

Character cannot be developed in ease and quiet.
Only through experience of trial and suffering
can the soul be strengthened, ambition inspired,
and success achieved.
Helen Keller

Out of suffering have emerged the
strongest souls. The most massive
characters are seared with scars.
Kahlil Gibran

L et's be dead honest. If we're going to be good at anything in life, we must be willing to endure the heat, pressure, suffering, time, trials, tribulations and scars to cast us into the most precious of gems, a diamond. Simply hoping, wishing or praying to be excellent isn't going to cut it. We've simply got to do the work.

Once upon a time in America there was a work ethic, an understanding that to achieve anything substantive one had to work at it for a good amount of time. This is a logical point of view. If one wants to be a classical performing pianist, for example, one has to practice hours each day for years to achieve a standard of excellence sufficient enough to play before an audience and then keep on practicing during one's performance years to keep the skills honed and alive. The famed Polish concert pianist, Ignacy Paderewski, said:

> *If I miss one day's practice, I notice it.*
> *If I miss two days, the critics notice it.*
> *If I miss three days, the audience notices it.*

Underscoring this commentary on work ethic reality, the famous 19th/20th Century Indian Saint, Sawan Singh, astutely noted: *If a dog walks through a cotton field, he does not come out dressed in a suit.*

Yet, in today's world there exists the unnatural belief that excellence can be had with no work, no effort, no struggle. And this is exactly what it is, unnatural. The natural order of things, like the creation of a diamond . . . or a classical pianist . . . or a Black Belt, takes enormous time, dedication, determination, sweat, blood, tears and years of applied effort. Trying to circumvent the process is impossible. If anyone thinks he or she is going to be a top quality artisan in any art without working at it, such a person is operating in a world of delusion. Sadly, suffering from delusion is a common ailment. 17th/18th Century, Saint Dariya of Bihar noted: *The whole world is overpowered by delusion. The delusion is overpowered by none.* Certainly one great delusion is thinking we can be transformed from common old chunks of coal into a radiant diamond, the most precious of all gems, without being subjected to heat, pressure and time - enormous amounts of time, enormous amounts of heat, enormous amounts of pressure.

In relation to our character becoming diamond-like, the famous Helen Keller factually remarks:

> *Character cannot be developed in ease and quiet.*
> *Only through experience of trial and suffering can*
> *the soul be strengthened, ambition inspired, and*
> *success achieved.*

If anyone knows what it's like to be a diamond, it's Helen Keller. Mark Twain once commented that of all the people in his life he would have liked to have met, one was Helen Keller. The other was Napoleon. This is the kind of stature this woman commanded. During her lifetime, she was a living legend on par with today's most noteworthy icons. She understood the depths of trial and long-suffering far beyond the common consciousness.

Khalil Gibran's statement is also profound:

Out of suffering have emerged the strongest souls.
The most massive characters are seared with scars.

What these august souls are stating is the relationship between work and excellence. We may want to achieve great things but we have to be realistic as to the process. Being deluded or having an instant-gratification mentally is not going to get the job done. If we want to transform ourselves and our talent from a common chunk of coal to a resplendent diamond, we simply have to endure the heat, pressure, time, study, practice, trials, tribulations, scars and suffering to get there. There is simply no other way.

#22

Perfect Speed

In the journey of accomplishment
the wise this adage heed --
fast or slow is not of note,
of note is *Perfect Speed.*

Impatience is wanting something to happen
before the due time.
Saint Charan Singh
[20th Century]

To every thing there is a season,
and a time to every purpose
under the heaven.
[Bible: Ecclesiastes 3:1]

You win battles by knowing the enemy's timing,
and using a timing which the enemy does not expect.
Miyamoto Musashi
[Famed Japanese Swordsmen-16th/17th Century]

In life, as it is in fighting, timing is everything. Once a fighter understands timing, the potential of his victories will soar, as reflected in the statement of Miyamoto Musashi, one of the greatest and most renowned swordsmen of his day and author of *The Book of Five Rings*, his flagship work on strategy, tactics, and philosophy.

Timing, however, must be perfect. Some timings may be very fast; others quite slow; still others erratic and broken. The essential thing in timing is to understand *perfect speed* which is *that speed allowing perfect execution*. Whether the movement is defensive or offensive, the timing and speed must be perfect to fit the situation.

Imagine swinging a baseball bat as soon as the ball leaves the pitcher's hand; swinging a tennis racket after the ball has passed the end line; stopping your car at a green light; closing your mouth before the spoon gets there with the soup; studying for a test after the test has been given and worst of all, telling someone you love them after they've died. Bad timing, right? Now assume your timing is perfect and you swing the bat at the right time, knocking the ball out of the stadium; you hit the tennis ball for a down-the-line winner; you stop at a red light and continue through a green light, as you should; you open your mouth as the spoon gets there; study for the test before you take it, and most critically of all, you inform that special someone that you love them before they pass on. Good timing, yes? Of course. Fighting is timing; life is timing, and success in both fighting and life is a matter of perfect timing, perfect speed - executing whatever it is that needs doing at the exact time it needs to be done to insure success.

True story. As a beginning martial artist, I didn't know much about the technical aspects of fighting. I was taught to be tough, hang in there, do your best - all the normal encouragement phrases but nothing really technical, and certainly nothing about timing.

As my fighting experience progressed throughout my karate journey, I got my rump kicked and head handed to me on a platter so many times I thought I had lost both at one time. My only fighting education during those days was in the school of hard knocks . . . hard kicks . . . hard punches . . . hard backfists and hard falls - all replete with bumps, bruises, cuts, broken bones and stitches. There seemed to be no end to the butt whoopin' I was receiving in those days, especially from Bob "Trucker" MacFarlane, a Black Belt buddy who used to clean my clock on a regular basis. I don't think I ever scored on him once. He was always kind about it and generous in his praise for me, but time and again he would tag me with one of his patented blazing fast backfists. His defenses were impenetrable. Thank goodness his control was immaculate. It should also be said that Bob MacFarlane was and is as great a gentlemen as he is a fighter.

At one stretch in my learning process, I even had one hundred fighting techniques memorized in groups of twenty-five which I could recall in a few seconds, thinking that a large number of techniques was the answer. It wasn't. Eventually what I discovered in my learning-to-fight-by-getting-my-head-handed-to-me-on-a-silver-platter strategy was that I didn't need all those techniques. All I needed was to make my attacks at the right *time*. When I learned this, I was able to reduce the number of techniques I was using from one hundred to a half-dozen! Truly. That's it. It was an amazing transition and became my greatest Ah-ha! moment in learning to fight. Miyamoto Musashi is absolutely right: *You win battles by knowing the enemy's timing, and using a timing which the enemy does not expect.*

Since martial arts is life, for us to be successful it's important we study the timing of life, the "when" of our actions. However, it's just as important to understand the "when not" to do something. Knowing *when not* to act is just as critical as knowing *when* to act. Attack or counter-attack at the right time and victory is assured. Attack or counter-attack at the wrong time and defeat is certain. The key in timing is to understand *perfect speed, that speed which allows us to execute perfectly.* And for those fighters who believe blinding speed is always the answer, the answer to that is that *the essential thing is not excessive speed, it is perfect speed.* When we understand this concept functionally, our fighting, as well as our life, will improve dramatically.

#23
Maximize The Minimum

To not get drained and tired,

and not be madly dumb,

in all things great and small

we must *Maximum the Minimum.*

There can be economy only where there is efficiency.
Benjamin Disraeli
[British Prime Minister-19th Century]

The highest type of efficiency is that which can
utilize existing material to the best advantage.
Jawaharlal Nehru
[Prime Minister of India - 20th Century]

There are only two qualities in the world:
efficiency and inefficiency, and only two sorts
of people: the efficient and the inefficient.
George Bernard Shaw

For any task, especially that of fighting or performing, we only have so much gas in the tank, and our success will be determined by how we manage the fuel, the energy in our tank. Therefore, to optimize the potential of success, we must *Maximize the Minimum*.

In order to function properly the body needs nutrition. With the extraordinary energy levels associated with any physically demanding performance, especially fighting, what is the number one nutrient the body needs to sustain itself and insure success? Carbohydrates? Protein? Water? Don't know? The answer is oxygen. More than any other nutritional element, people involved in physically demanding activities need oxygen. Yes, of course it is also the number one element needed to sustain life, but it is critical to an athlete, especially a martial artist/fighter whose well-being depends on his skills of combat; skills which, if deactivated due to a lack of oxygen, can have disastrous results. Therefore, when engaging in strenuous exercise or combat, we must be able to maximize the minimum amount of oxygen we have. If we run out too soon, it's curtains.

Arguably, the number one impediment to maximizing the minimum amount of oxygen usage in the body is tension. Why? Because tension - both mental and physical, burns up oxygen at an enormous rate. Without exception, a beginning fighter will burn out in a few minutes of combat whereas a well-trained fighter will last ten times longer. The difference between the novice and the expert fighter is that the expert has learned how to manage his energy expenditure; in effect, *maximizing the minimum.*

The question then arises, "How do we manage tension?" We manage tension through relaxation. Okay, so the next question is, "How do we manage relaxation?" We manage relaxation in two primary ways: 1. mind control, and 2. technical expertise.

When analyzed, we realize that much tension is directly linked to our mind and its processes. For example, a baseball, tennis or golf coach may say to a player, "Hit the ball harder." A soccer coach may say to his player, "Kick the ball harder." A novice martial arts teacher may say to his pupil, "Hit the target harder." For most beginners the reaction to hitting, kicking or punching the ball or target harder equates to tightening the muscles before hitting the ball or striking the target. This is the exact opposite of what should be done. Tension destroys relaxation, compromising speed and technique. When speed and technique are compromised, power is comprised and the result is a weak and often clumsy hit, kick or strike, not a powerful one. And this lack of power and proper execution begins in the mind. When the mind hears the word, "harder," it often equates that word to "stronger," and failure follows. *Harder* doesn't equal *stronger*.

Mental stress can also create tension. How often have employees or students developed tension headaches because of stress? Too many to count for sure. Yet, tension-generated stress and its subsequent physical manifestations such as headaches, can be remedied in the mind because ultimately, when we think about it, it is the mind reacting to the stimuli that causes the tension and its subsequent ailments. In effect, what has happened is that we have allowed an outside external stimulus to affect us. The fault lies in us not controlling ourselves, not in the stimulus or stimuli.

This may seem an unfair statement to make, but it is true. We're not victims when we experience tension headaches. Frankly, we're the cause because we did not control or neutralize the incoming energy as efficiently as we could have, whether that energy resulted from a boss being too demanding, projects coming due, tests lurking on the horizon or any number of other possibilities. These so-called causes are all neutral and not causes at all. We're the ones who translate them into stress, and therefore we're the cause of the effects, i.e., headaches. Once we understand this link between ourselves and the outside world, we can manage the outcome more efficiently and healthfully. Remember, *this is our life; it is our responsibility.* We can't control other people, events or circumstances extraneous to us but we can control how we respond to such things. *Control is the mark of a master*, and if we're going to master ourselves and our life, we must master energies and influences bombarding us from the outside world and not allow them to control us. If we do allow them to control us, we, not they, are the cause.

The second way to manage relaxation is through technical expertise. This aspect demands we learn our craft and know how to execute every part of it while using the least amount of energy needed to perform the task. To learn efficiently, begin by executing each move, whatever it is, slowly and in a relaxed manner. Gradually increase speed while remaining relaxed. If you tense up, start over. It's important to develop technique that is both correct and relaxed. Keep practicing . . . perfectly, until the desired results are achieved. In this way we can help *maximum the minimum.*

#24

Perfect Practice

Perfect Practice

Perfect practice, perfect makes.
Simple practice makes a habit.
If it's perfection we desire,
then we must make *Perfection* habit.

Simple habits, habits make.
The outcome of our loves
becomes extraordinary in the law
that *perfect is as perfect does.*

When we spend time in forming
those things we want in 'grooves',
then we must practice perfectly
for *perfect is as perfect moves.*

We can't expect perfection
from results our effort takes,
if we don't practice perfectly,
for *perfect is as perfect makes.*

Be thou perfect.
Bible - Genesis 17:1

Perfection is attained by slow degrees;

it requires the hand of time.

Voltaire

There is such a thing as perfection . . .

and our purpose for living is to find

that perfection and show it forth.

The gull sees farthest who flies highest.

Richard Bach
Jonathan Livingston Seagull

God's work is permanent and everlasting

and exists in a state of perfection in every man.

Man is the top of all creation, the perfect handiwork

of Nature in all aspects. He contains within himself the key

to unlock the mystery of the Universe and to contact the Creator.

It is the greatest and the highest good fortune of any sentient

being to be born in the form of man.

Saint Jagat Singh
[20th Century]

Perfect is he who, by practice and meditation, lifts
his soul to its real abode, freeing it from all
bonds both internal and external, gross,
subtle and causal and thus detaches
his mind from the world and
its phenomena.

Swami Ji Maharaj

[19th Century Saint]

W e've all heard the phrase, *practice makes perfect.* In reality, practice doesn't make perfect. Practice only makes a habit. *Perfect practice makes perfect.*

Philosophically, there exist a vast number of people who do not believe perfection is possible; in other words, it is unattainable. Their belief is that no one is perfect and therefore we live in a state of personal imperfection. Thus, not only do their beliefs define them, their lives and accomplishments, they limit them and keep them from experiencing perfection or striving to achieve it. The phrase, *argue for your limitations and, sure enough, they're yours,* [Richard Bach] is a perfect match for those with this philosophy.

It is true we all have flaws but that does not mean we will always have flaws, especially when considering the grand scope of all life and its spiritual ramifications. If God commands, *Be thou perfect*, who are we to argue otherwise?

By taking a stand for imperfection by acknowledging we all have flaws is to excuse our flaws and assume, erroneously, we'll always have them. Such philosophy also sets the bar very low. The truth is that we will continue to have flaws and operate at a low level unless we work to correct our flaws and climb to a higher level. But this takes work, a lot of work and concentrated effort, and those individuals exhibiting a weak disposition and inability to accept the challenge will naturally avoid and argue against the perfection-oriented philosophy. This is one critical argument for martial arts training: it teaches us to be warriors, to engage and conquer both internal and external challenges. Martial arts training should teach the soul that he or she is strong, courageous and capable of anything, perfection included. Martial arts training teaches us how to fight and conquer, not just people, but negative, outworn and limiting thoughts and concepts.

The highest of spiritual teachings exhorts us to be perfect. Therefore, strive for perfection. You may not hit the mark in this life, but it's a sure bet that if you don't aim for the target, you'll never hit it, and Perfect Spiritual Masters, not humans, tell us perfection is possible if we keep our nose to the grindstone and our eye to the Light.

As we move toward perfection our personal power increases, eventually leading to a state of perfection in higher spiritual regions. But if we don't work to perfection, we'll never advance and will never get "there." To some, this thought of higher realms of existence may seem esoteric, and to others strange and weird. Yet, what is strange and weird is this world with its cavalcade of limiting, negative and incarcerating thought.

As those of us know who study martial arts and who have devoted our lives to it, we advance from level to level, eventually surpassing any concept of belt ranks and simply continue in our journey to know more, study more, do more, succeed more, elevate more, be more. Once we get to a certain level of training, belt ranks don't mean anything to us. We transcend the belt motif. Obviously, we begin at the white belt "region" and gradually attain higher and higher levels of expertise. The learning is never over. It never stops. There is always more to know and higher regions to evolve to in relation to our martial arts knowledge and ability. The higher we climb, the better, the more perfect we become. We get to the top not by accepting our flaws, weaknesses, shortcomings and limitations but rather by learning and struggling to overcome them and . . . we eventually succeed.

As we go through the ranks, we become more perfect in the process. If we had assumed from the beginning that we were imperfect and so full of flaws and weaknesses that we could never get to the top, then we wouldn't. This is why some people never make it to a black belt level. They don't believe they can; they buy into their own weaknesses and limitations or allow themselves to be victimized by the negative and limiting thoughts of others who couldn't make it and wanted company in their confinement and, guess what, they become the manifestation of their beliefs, or worse yet, someone else's! Astonishing, isn't it? Actually, it's natural. We are what we think, and if we think we can't, we can't. If we think we can, we can and do. If we believe perfection is impossible, we will find a way to support it or entertain the beliefs of other people who are also perfection-challenged.

Therefore, as a martial artist, or any artist, when we practice our art, we should always and relentlessly do our utmost to practice perfectly. Simply practicing does not insure success. Practice only makes a habit and that habit can be good or bad. To insure the ever-increasing quality of our own art, we must endlessly work to achieve perfection. Why be mediocre? Why remain stagnant just because someone with a limited understanding of life said it's impossible to be perfect? Nonsense. As a practicing martial artist, or any artist in any discipline, your own experience should prove to you the ever-ascending quality of unlimited expression. Remember, *The gull sees farthest who flies highest*!

#25

Concentration
Coalesces

Perfect Masters throughout time,

in all of their addresses,

state that in pursuit of truth

Concentration Coalesces.

If you don't concentrate, you'll end up on your rear.
Tai Babilonia

To be able to concentrate for a considerable time
is essential to difficult achievement.
Bertrand Russell

The stages of the Noble Path are: Right View, Right Thought,
Right Speech, Right Behavior, Right Livelihood,
Right Effort, Right Mindfulness and
Right Concentration.
Buddha

To *coalesce* means to merge or fuse into a single point. The importance of concentration to success in life's endeavors has already been addressed in the vignette *Concentration is the First Key*. In martial arts this fusing into one point involves the body, mind and spirit.

Okay, the importance of concentration has been stated but, one may ask, "How is concentration achieved?" Excellent question. Following is one way to help develop concentration. It involves a game called, *Integration*.

The game of *Integration* involves bringing together our body, mind and spirit to a place of one-pointedness. It is a simple game but difficult to conquer. Once conquered, one's ability to concentrate and receive the untold benefits of awesome concentration will begin to reveal themselves in the day-to-day activities of life. When we play the game, however, we soon learn how difficult concentration is, as well as how the three integral parts of the game - the body, mind and spirit - interact.

The game of *Integration* has three phases, each phase being more difficult and challenging than the first. And this is only the first version of the game. More difficult and challenging renditions can be easily created, but this first version will suffice for now. The three phrases of *Integration* are:

Phase 1. Simple Number Counting

Phase 2. See and Say

Phase 3. Overlay

Phase 1: Simple Number Counting

1. Schedule some quiet time, perhaps 5 to 15 minutes.

2. Sit or lay down. It's best to sit. Laying down may put you to sleep.

3. Once in position, you cannot move. You must remain still for the entire exercise. If you move, you lose and must start the game over. Remaining perfectly still is the first major rule of the game in all its phases. This includes moving your head, fingers, hands, arms, or any body part. Scratching, itching or wiping drops of perspiration from your forehead are disallowed. You must remain perfectly still.

4. With your eyes closed, mentally begin counting from one to ten. Concentrate only on the numbers. If your mind wanders and you begin thinking about anything else, you lose and must restart the game at number one. Do this until you can count to ten with total focus and concentration. Once mastered, extend the end point to twenty, then thirty, forty, fifty, a hundred, two hundred and up to one thousand. Obviously, the longer the game, the more time you will need during your "sitting." However, you must abide by the two major rules of the game:

    1. You cannot move and must remain perfectly still.

    2. If your mind wanders and you begin thinking about anything else, you lose, and must restart the game. Keep playing until your concentration becomes strong enough to reach an end point of one thousand.

This exercise teaches us several things immediately:

1. How difficult it is for the body to remain still.
2. How difficult it is for the mind to remain still.
3. How easily the mind slips into other thoughts.
4. How our ability to concentrate needs strengthening.
5. How we are more than just our mind and body.
6. How powerful and deceptive the mind is as an opponent.
7. How developed our skills are as a true warrior.

Phase 2: See and Say

1. Same method and rules as before:
    *   Quiet space
    *   Quiet time [15 to 30 minutes]
    *   You move, you lose. Start over.
    *   Your mind wanders, you lose. Start over.
2. This time you will *see* each number in your mind's eye and then *say* the number silently to yourself. Hence, "See and Say." So . . . in your mind see the number 1. As you focus on it, say "one." Then see the number 2 and say "two." Then the number 3, say it and so forth. This phase will be more challenging because two variables are used: sight and silent sound. The first attempt can be from one to ten. When this is mastered, move to twenty, thirty, etc. as before. If your focus slips and your mind wanders, as it most likely will, start over until you achieve the appropriate goal. Keep pushing the number barrier backwards.

Phase 3: Overlay

1. Same method and rules as before:
   - Quiet space
   - Quiet time [15 to 30 minutes or longer]
   - You move, you lose. Start over.
   - Your mind wanders, you lose. Start over.

2. This phase is even more challenging.

   You will begin the game by seeing the number 1 as before. However, rather than saying its number, you will silently say a phrase or catalogue of words laid over the number, hence, *overlay*. It can be anything you want. As an example, we'll use the belt ranking order of the Karate Institute of America which is: white, yellow, orange, purple, blue, green brown, black and back to white, thus taking us full circle. Therefore, see the number 1 and silently say the words: "white - yellow - orange - purple - blue - green - brown - black - white" and then move to number 2. Repeat the same phrase or catalogue you've chosen to use. Continue in sequential order to ten, twenty, thirty, a hundred, two hundred, a thousand. If you can get to a thousand without your mind slipping out, you have excellent concentration.

   What do these exercises teach us? One of the first things we realize is how restless the mind and body are, particularly as the game is extended in time and difficulty. The mind doesn't want to be still at all and will use any opportunity to move away from the discipline we seek to impose upon it. With the mind behaving in this manner, we learn that we are not our mind but something else. If we were our mind, we would be able to control ourselves, right? But in this exercise, even though we dictate the rules - that the body cannot move and the mind cannot wander, the latter wanders with ease and the body wants to and most likely will in time.

As we soon learn in this series of drills, concentration is a difficult skill to master. Enter our spirit, our will. As the game progresses in difficulty and time, our will must engage the battle and move to the forefront. If it's weak, we must strengthen it because it will help us strengthen our mind, which is a wild child, to say the least. All it wants to do is play around and not be held to task. In fact, when being disciplined, it revolts and it is quite good at its job. The body is easier to control in the beginning but after a while it, too, can't stand the stillness and cries out to move and be active. It is at this point we learn the definition of what it is to be a true warrior. Enter the forces of discipline, determination, courage.

Through this game of *Integration* we are given another tool for integrating our body, mind and spirit represented by the triangle, the symbol of perfection. Please don't feel you have to be successful immediately. Frankly, the game is a life-long process from cradle to grave. Such is the journey of life, success and spiritual ascent.

#26

Y.O.Y.O.

From birth to death the truth be known,

when you cry tears

You're On Your Own.

If you're attacked when all alone,

the truth remains --

You're On Your Own.

Fair weather friends have always flown.

When your fame dies,

You're On Your Own.

So best to seek the sanctum

of the Journey headed Home

from this wasteland of the loveless

where *You Are On Your Own.*

The strongest man in the world is he who stands most alone.

Henrik Ibsen

I am sure of this, that by going much alone a man will get

more of a noble courage in thought and word than

from all the wisdom that is in books.

Ralph Waldo Emerson

We must learn to live with ourselves,
independently of anything in this world.
Saint Charan Singh

I never must forget that none's my true
companion here, for all are
gathered here for selfish ends.
Saint Kabir

Regarding worldly relationship, it may be pointed out
that all relationships are based on selfish motives on this
material plane. Husbands, brothers, wives, sisters, other
relatives and friends are attached to us because of the
advantages that accrue to them from us and are apt to
cool down in their zeal and love towards us when they
feel that we are of no use to them. Do not expect much
from them but do your duty towards them and care for
them even if they fail to reciprocate your love.
Saint Jagat Singh

Solitude

Ella Wheeler Wilcox

Laugh, and the world laughs with you;
Weep, and you weep alone;
For the sad old earth must borrow its mirth,
But has trouble enough of its own.
Sing, and the hills will answer;
Sigh, it is lost on the air;
The echoes bound to a joyful sound,
But shrink from voicing care.

Rejoice, and men will seek you;
Grieve, and they turn and go;
They want full measure of all your pleasure,
But they do not need your woe.
Be glad, and your friends are many;
Be sad, and you lose them all,—
There are none to decline your nectared wine,
But alone you must drink life's gall.

Feast, and your halls are crowded;
Fast, and the world goes by.
Succeed and give, and it helps you live,
But no man can help you die.
There is room in the halls of pleasure
For a large and lordly train,
But one by one we must all file on
Through the narrow aisles of pain.

The Black Belt Book of Life   King

It may be a difficult fact to accept but the reality of life, and certainly the reality of being attacked, is that *You're On Your Own*, the acronym for which is Y.O.Y.O.

Ella Wheeler Wilcox expressed this beautifully in her poem "Solitude" above. The quotes from Saints Charan Singh, Kabir and Jagat Singh corroborate life in this world, and while we'd all like to think and believe we have many friends and loved ones, in actuality we only have ourselves and God. For all intents and purposes, we're born alone, we live alone and we die alone.

At no time is this more poignant than if we have to defend ourselves. How devastating it can be to be in fear for your life and have people you thought were your friends turn tail and high tail it out of harm's way, leaving you to fight the fight . . . alone. If this has happened to you, you understand the illusory depth of so-called friendship. Occasionally, there exists the true friend who will stand and fight with you, support you, be there for you, but such friends are rare indeed. And this is okay because in the final analysis, this is *our life and it is our responsibility*. We need to fight our own battles. Therefore, we need to be strong and courageous warriors. It's no other person's duty to protect us or be there for us, or put themselves in harm's way for us, and wisdom dictates we not only understand this but also the distinct probability that in a self-defense situation we will be totally on our own. Know though, that in our own ascent, when we attain levels of consciousness that others have never touched, and fly in skies in which others have never flown, we will, like Jonathan Livingston Seagull, experience that joy, deservedly, on our own.

#27

The Way Out Is In

Life is full of problems,

and when they settle in,

remember, for solutions,

The Way Out is In.

We can't solve problems by using the same kind

of thinking we used when we created them.

Dr. Albert Einstein

Every problem has a gift for you in its hands.

Richard Bach

No problem can stand the assault of sustained thinking.

Voltaire

Don't tell your problems to people: eighty percent

don't care; and the other twenty percent

are glad you have them.

Lou Holtz

In learning a new basic skill, technique or tactic, one of the best ways to really get to know it is to get inside it and pick it apart from as many angles as possible. We can't learn something by not committing ourselves to it. We must delve deeply into it. The same is true for any problem or issue in life. The way out of the dilemma is directly into it. Hence the phrase, *The Way Out is In*.

This may seem a logical solution, but often one choice in solving problems for some people is to run away, avoid or hide from them. This does nothing to actually solve the problems and can actually make them worse. How, for example, can a person learn to fight if he doesn't place himself in a combative environment and engage his opponent? Studying theory only goes so far in the education process. We need real-world experience. Getting in a ring, facing a challenger, butting heads, clashing fists, forearms, elbows, knees and feet and staring into the onslaught of an oncoming attack is the only way to truly learn how to fight.

The same is true for any activity. If you want to learn how to ride a horse, you've eventually got to saddle up, get on and ride. Sure you may get bucked off or thrown off, but how else can you truly learn? Watching from outside the corral surely won't get the job done.

True story. Mark was a great horseman. The things this man could do with a horse were phenomenal. People from far and wide would send him their problem horses to be trained or retrained. Yet, Mark's knowledge didn't come from books. It came at a steep and often dangerous price.

In learning to ride bucking horses, Mark once got bucked off the same horse eight times in fifteen minutes. Was he crazy to keep getting back on? That's debatable. However, when asked why he kept getting back on knowing that he would probably get thrown off again, he said it was the only way he could learn how to ride a bucking horse. He had to learn why he was getting bucked off, what he was doing wrong. It wasn't his ego he was chasing, but knowledge. Mark's solution to the problem of learning how to ride bucking horses was not to run away from the problem, but rather to dive straight into it. For Mark, *the way out was in*, and this problem-solving ability created a solid reputation for him as the man to see when it came to training horses. There was no better.

Another true story. Anna "Wildcat" Griffin is one of the toughest people you'll ever know. She's a Kiado-Ryu Black Belt now, an excellent fighter and martial artist, but it wasn't always that way. As a teenager with a brown belt ranking, she would spar with the brown and black belt men. One night during a match she got knocked out, cold. Her parents were informed and she was able to get home without incident. What is amazing is the very next night, Anna was back in the ring fighting . . . again, after being knocked out just twenty-four hours earlier! Grown men have quit karate after getting slightly clipped on the nose, let alone knocked out, but not Anna. She's as tough as her "Wildcat" handle implies.

Like Mark, the thing with Anna was that she knew the only way for her to learn how to fight was to get back in the ring immediately and learn what she did wrong so she could remedy the problem and improve her skills so she wouldn't get clocked again. Not only is she brave and courageous, she's smart, tough, wise and definitely not a quitter. Anna "Wildcat" Griffin is the stuff substantive people are made of. Such a tribute. Such a Black Belt. Her brother, James "Psycho" Griffin, also a Kiado-Ryu Black Belt, is no less courageous. Two tough individuals, brother and sister, from the same family is amazing and a tribute to their parents for raising them to be independent, strong, courageous.

Of course there are countless stories of individuals like Mark, Anna and James in all walks of life whose solution to a problem is to attack it at its very core, in spite of the consequences. They know the way out of their problem is ironically directly into it. It takes courage to manage life in this way, but the great ones do it because they know that in relation to life's many problems, the solution is to apply the adage, *the way out is in.*

#28

Peace At Any Price Is
Not Peace, It's Slavery

Living trapped within your self

certainly isn't savory;

Peace at any price is not peace,

it's slavery.

Better to starve free than be a fat slave.

Aesop

If slavery is not wrong, nothing is wrong.

Abraham Lincoln

No man is entitled to the blessings of freedom

unless he be vigilant in its preservation.

General Douglas MacArthur

The moment the slave resolves that he will

no longer be a slave, his fetters fall.

Gandhi

Everything in life has its price. The price of freedom is the greatest price of all because there is nothing greater than freedom - the right to live as we choose without interference from outside forces and sources as long as we do not infringe upon the rights of others. Untold numbers of souls have fought and died to preserve their freedom and that of those they love. Certainly, as General Douglas MacArthur succinctly and eloquently stated: *No man is entitled to the blessings of freedom unless he be vigilant in its preservation.*

Contrarily, there is nothing worse than slavery, whether we are subjected by another or trapped within the confines of our separate prisons, stuck to its walls by shackles of our own making, forced to eat the fruit of the seeds and deeds we planted.

Freedom must be fought for . . . every moment of every day with our will, our discipline, mind, body and, if necessary, the physical and material tools of self-defense. If we're opposed to defend our life, our freedom, our values, then we can blame no one but ourselves if they are taken from us, as they most certainly will be if we refuse to protect them. Even if we have to fight to preserve our life and our freedom and we die in the process, at least we died having fought for something meaningful. In doing so, we would not have died in vain. It is far better to die preserving life and freedom than to live in vain and shame for submitting to the chains of enslavement.

Pythagoras said, *No man is free who cannot control himself.* Therefore, freedom begins with our own discipline, self-control, right thought and right action. Great freedom demands great sacrifice in the form of persistent discipline. As the famous American actress, Katharine Hepburn said, *Without discipline, there's no life at all.* Discipline is the crux of success. Without it there is no control, and without control there is no freedom, only the potential of slavery.

Too often, people operate under the premise that peace should be maintained at all costs? All costs? Would you give up your life to an attacker to maintain his peace? If you don't value yourself or your life, then what is your life worth? What are your values worth? If you're a woman and some predator wants to rape you and take away your dignity, health and well-being and you believe that by being passive and allowing him to have his way with you, you will acquire peace, you won't. On a personal note, in my martial arts career I have seen the effects of rape. They're horrible, often crippling women for the rest of their lives, not to mention the lives of those they love and who love them.

There is an erroneous belief that peace equates to passivity. This is incorrect. Peace is not passivity. Peace is an active state of balance between the opposing polarities of passivity on the one hand and activity on the other.

To understand this, let's use cancer as an example. In one sense, cancer is a passively growing disease. If we equated peace with passivity, then we would say that cancer is a peaceful disease. Nothing could be further from the truth. If cancer gets out of control, violent measures may have to be used to destroy it - chemotherapy, radiation, surgery. These are violent measures but necessary in order to bring the individual back into a state of balance and peace. The moral of the story: peace sometimes demands great and violent action to preserve it, just as if one had to defend his life from someone who wanted to destroy it. If we acquiesce under threat of harm by believing that peace at such a price will bring peace, then our delusion will enslave us and we will deserve exactly what we get . . . slavery.

All decent people want peace. The rub is that there can never be peace in *this* world because of its polarized nature of opposites: positive/negative, light/dark, up/down, back/forth, hot/cold, day/night, man/woman, yin/yang, and on and on and on. In a teeter-totter world, struggle is the way of life because we're always fighting to maintain our balance, as well we should, and must to have a fulfilled life. It is because of the intrinsic nature of this world that 20th Century Master, Charan Singh, admonished people to, *Just live in the creation and get out of it.* Out of it? Yes. Mystic teachings explain that other worlds, other mansions, other realms exist that are beyond the physical plane, which is where we are currently living. To learn more about these mystic teachings, read *Messages from the Masters: Timeless Truths for Spiritual Seekers* available at www.richardking.net.

The thing of note in the mundane world is that if we want peace, we must be willing to fight for it. To sell whatever we own, including our freedom and lives, in hopes of creating peace will not work, ever. Peace cannot be created through pacification if someone is bent on taking our life. We must sometimes unfortunately fight to preserve a life of peace because *peace at any price is not peace, it is slavery.*

#29

Grown Ups, Own Up

In living life from birth to death
and in the filling of its cup,
responsible people realize that
Grown Ups, Own Up.

Responsibility is the price of greatness.
Churchill

If you want to cut your own throat,
don't come to me for a bandage.
Margaret Thatcher

Let everyone sweep in front of his own door,
and the whole world will be clean.
Goethe

You are responsible for yourself.
You are not responsible for the world.
Saint Charan Singh

We are all responsible for our own actions, accountable for everything we have done, are doing, will do or have failed to do. This is an irrefutable fact of life and no social convention or passing mindset, however much cherished by the masses, can alter this truth. If we are grown up, we own up to our life, our choices and their consequences. Pointing a finger of blame at others for our actions is not only wrong, it is degrading to us because it speaks directly to our lack of character.

Besides, when we point a blaming finger at someone else for things we've done we must not overlook the fact that three of our own fingers are pointing back at us, reminding us in a three-fold capacity that we are the one to blame.

The 3 Fingers of Blame

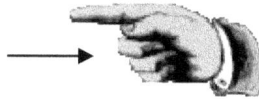

Notice where they're pointing.

This principle of self-accountability has been heavily under siege through the last few decades of the 20th Century into the first decade of the 21st Century and there seems to be little diminution of its lack of application. There is an infestation of non-accountability spreading like wildfire in our culture, an infectious disease destroying the nobility of man, and the disconcerting part of it is there seems to be little concern about its proliferation. The idea of hurting people's feelings takes precedence over one's character, and when feelings trump character, there is strong reason for concern. Honestly, what's more important, one's character or one's feelings?

For example, if we're overweight, it's no one else's fault but our own. We're the one who puts the food in our mouth, fails to exercise and take proper care of our God-given bodies. It's not the fault of the fast-food chains serving huge portions of food loaded with fat and sugar and supported by slick advertising campaigns. Are we helpless automatons devoid of any semblance of self-control or thought about what we're ingesting? Are we dogs on a leash, moving here and there, totally under the command of the leash master?

If we're addicted to drugs or alcohol, is it someone else's fault? We made the original choice to put ourselves in a position to become involved with these poisons. If we hurt, injure or kill someone while under their influence, is it the fault of the alcohol and drug companies and their relentless marketing machines? Notwithstanding the nefarious nature of these poison peddlers whose focus is not on the health and well-being of people but on their own bank accounts, we can't blame our usage on them or on anything or anyone else. Certainly, we cannot claim innocence.

If we physically harm someone because our temper gets out of control, it's not their fault, it's ours. Nor is it the fault of society, our background, parents, the weather or the government. If we're adults, the buck stops with us and we, not anyone else, are responsible and accountable for our actions. There simply are no excuses. *Grown-ups, own up.*

The Black Belt Book of Life   King

Martial arts training is an excellent vehicle for teaching accountability. Whether we're sparring, performing katas/forms [choreographed routines], practicing self-defense techniques or extemporaneous attack drills, we are totally and completely responsible for what we do, and if we hurt someone else or become hurt, it's our fault, plainly and simply. If we injure a fellow student, ninety-nine percent of the time it is because of a lack of our own self-control, faulty technique, lack of care for the other person or an unrestrained ego on the prowl to prove its silly superiority. Contrarily, if we get hurt, invariably it's because we didn't move when we should have, missed a block or parry we should have made, lost our balance or our concentration. Ultimately, we are the reason for injury and our finger should be pointed at us, not someone else.

At the Karate Institute of America we have a standing rule: *if you get hurt, it's your fault.* No pointing fingers at anyone else, especially during fighting. If you chose to engage; you must accept responsibility for what happens in the engagement. Children [of all ages] make excuses for their behavior. Adults do not . . . or rather should not. *Grown ups, own up.* This is the way of life, and for the individual who seeks a sense of self-worth and dignity, there is no other option. Is this tough love? Perhaps it is, but it is only directed to those whose characters are still in the growing-into-adulthood stage. Hopefully, the adulthood stage comes sooner than later.

#30

Adapt or Die

In the day-to-day battles of life,

we can weep or laugh or cry,

but the indefensible truth

is that we either *Adapt or Die.*

The wise adapt themselves to circumstances,

as water molds itself to the pitcher.

Chinese Proverb

Fixed fortifications are monuments to man's stupidity.

General George Patton Jr.

The nature of war is ceaseless change . . .

It is one of the most important tasks of command

to effect timely and proper change of tactics.

Sun Tzu

All fixed set patterns are incapable of

adaptability or pliability. The truth is

outside of all fixed patterns.

Bruce Lee

Life changes . . . ceaselessly. War changes . . . ceaselessly. Battles change . . . ceaselessly. It is a fact of life that one of the true constants in life is change. Like the waters of the ocean and their tides upon the shore, change is the order of the moment.

Adaptation. It is the antidote to change and critical to survival. Whether it is applied to life, war, personal battles, family situations or geographical occurrences, being able to adapt is the key to survival and success for any living species.

To adapt means to adjust. Therefore, the principle of adjustment is central to our well-being. If we're too fixed, too stuck, too locked into our own ways of being or to a mindset that will not bend, the result can't be good.

Warriors such as the famed Sun Tzu, Bruce Lee, George Patton and all great generals understand these principles as deeply as anyone, if not more, because in their worlds life is the cost of their inability to adapt. If they are not adaptable in war, many soldiers will die, a major concern, especially if one has a conscience.

This inability to adjust was no more obvious than in the 1991 Gulf War between Allied Military Forces led by General Norman Schwarzkopf against Iraqi leader, Saddam Hussein, who claimed that such a conflict would be the "Mother of all Battles." Although boldly labeled, it became instead the "Mother of all Defeats." In preparation to the Allied Forces' attack, Hussein entrenched his tanks, aiming them at a beachhead where he presumed the attack would start because of allied attack-landing rehearsals. But these rehearsals were all a ruse, a deception. This was a costly mistake for Hussein, who would have been well served to have studied warfare, especially paying attention to General George Patton's observation that *Fixed fortifications are monuments to man's stupidity.* Schwarzkopf faked a frontal attack on the beachhead and executed an "end run" around Hussein's entrenched armored defenses. This highly mobile flanking maneuver allowed the Allies to get behind Hussein's frontline fixed fortifications, laying waste to the Iraqi army in a mere 100 hours, initiating a re-titling of the "Mother of all Battles" to the "100 Hour War." Hussein was humiliated and defeated, a precursor to future events when Allied forces destroyed his murderous regime in 2003. Hussein was tried by his own people and died by hanging in 2006, ending his reign of terror.

This entire historic occurrence is a major example of one's inability to adapt. Hussein didn't or couldn't. He died. Perhaps he should have heeded the principle, *adapt or die.*

On the other side of the coin, especially during the Gulf War, the Allied Forces under the brilliant command of General Norman Schwarzkopf did adapt and they were victorious.

Such is the reality of life, war and battles. If we're to be successful in life, we must learn to adapt, adjust and modify our thoughts and actions as they apply to the circumstances at hand. How do we adapt? By being flexible, supple, like the branches of a willow tree. We need to *bend not break*, as the saying goes. This means we need to be open to change and modification. Having a strong will is good, but if it's too strong, too rigid, it will not be able to flex, and in that lack of flexion, it will collapse, like ill-constructed buildings in an earthquake. The same goes for our attitudes, principles, beliefs and concepts held dear, sometimes too dear. They must be flexible in all ways - mentally, emotionally, physically, financially. If we can't be flexible when circumstances demand, then we may well be victimized by our own inability to functionally understand the principle, *adapt or die.*

#31

Doing The Right Thing
Is The Right Thing
To Do

When confronted in life with options

and we wonder which option to choose,

there really is no other option:

Doing the right thing is the right thing to do.

Do what you should, not what you can.

Saint Charan Singh

The superior man understands what is right;

the inferior man understands what will sell.

Confucius

Do what you feel in your heart to be right - for you'll be criticized

anyway. You'll be damned if you do, and damned if you don't.

Eleanor Roosevelt

He has honor if he holds himself to an ideal

of conduct though it is inconvenient,

unprofitable, or dangerous to do so.

Walter Lippman

The Black Belt Book of Life   King

In this world where money, fame, name, power, position, celebrity and self-interest are rampant, it may be perplexing to know what to do when facing certain situations, especially if we're young and inexperienced in life. The answer, however, is simple. Regardless of the issue or problem at hand, the ethical person will always do the right thing because it's the right thing to do.

This begs the question, "What is the right thing to do? The right thing to do is the ethical thing, the spiritual thing, the honest thing, that thing that God would do. It's not a hard decision if we ask ourselves what we should do, listen to the answer and act on it. Oftentimes, however, our self-interest gets in the way and we end up serving ourselves rather than serving the highest and best good of the issue involved.

Saint Charan Singh says, *Do what you should, not what you can.* This is the spiritual solution. Yet, it's a fair bet to say that most people do what they can, not what they should. The typical business solution to making money is to "charge what the market will bear" and to serve the almighty "bottom line" of profitability regardless of the pain and hardship it causes others. This begs another question, "How much is too much?" How many CEOs and business tycoons charge inordinate amounts of money for things that people have to have for mere survival and for which people suffer greatly to purchase? Furthermore, how much do such CEOs take as compensation for their services? And is such compensation justified? How much money can one spend in a day?

Confucius says, *The superior man understands what is right;*

the inferior man understands what will sell. The "superior man" is he who has a spiritual and humanitarian foundation to his character and evaluates every situation for its ethical correctness first before considering its profitability. For example, are the alcohol, tobacco and drug industries doing what is right for the health and well-being of people or are they doing what serves their financial bottom line? The superior man would never do anything that would potentially harm, injure, debilitate or destroy another human being. The inferior man would and does do such things because his interests are for himself and himself only. Ultimately, his lack of compassion and right thought will be his undoing. In this world which operates under the great law of karma, what goes around comes around; what we sow, we reap; what we plant, we harvest; what we place onto the Circle of Life cycles back 'round to encircle us. It is an inescapable truth. Individuals who promote, market and distribute poisons and harmful products and services will one day be imprisoned by them. It's just a matter of time.

Of course we all know the golden rule: *Do unto others as you would have them do unto you.* This is a nice philosophy, but it's perceived to be just that, a nice philosophy. As it's written, there's no call to correct one's behavior or act in a specific way. However, when the law of karma is attached to this statement, it's truth rings more clear.

> *Do unto others as you would have them do unto you because as you do unto others, it shall be done unto you.*

When the second clause is added, it changes the entire understanding of the *golden rule* because it transforms it from a nice philosophy to an inescapable law, informing the doer of the action that what he does to others will be done to him. So if a person lies to another, he will be lied to. If he lies to a million people, he will eventually have to endure a million lies. If he hurts others or makes decisions that will hurt, endanger, maim or kill others; if he steals from them or lies to them, he will someday have to experience the same amount of negativity he perpetrated on others, whether his payment comes due in this life or future lives. Nobody escapes his actions. No one is above karmic law. We all have to pay for everything we do in life. Therefore, it is an extremely bad decision to do anything that hurts, damages, destroys or impacts others in a negative way.

Walter Lippman's comment is apropos:

He has honor if he holds himself to an ideal of conduct though it is inconvenient, unprofitable, or dangerous to do so.

In other words, the superior man does what is right, regardless of whether such action is convenient, profitable or safe for him. In our everyday actions can we say that we base our decisions on this ideal? Or do we consider what serves us first, with no thought as to how our decisions affect and impact others?

If we're to live a spiritual life, a moral life, an ethical life; if we're to express the highest ideals of what a human being can be, then when we're confronted with choices in this life it would be in keeping with life's highest ideals if we remembered that, *doing the right thing is the right thing to do.*

#32

We Compete to Test Our Skill, Not Expand Our Ego

In the game of sport,

of competition and friendly foe,

We compete to test our skill,

not expand our ego.

Ego is the biggest enemy of humans.

Rig-Veda

The world is a house of collyrium [an abode of evil];

a veritable well of the poison of egotism.

Guru Ravidas - 16th/17th Century Mystic

Learning increases ego instead of diminishing it

and takes us further away from the Lord.

Kabir - 16th/17th Century Mystic

Avoid having your ego so close to your position that

when your position falls, your ego goes with it.

Colin Powell

Ego is a great deterrent to the spiritual development of man, especially martial artists who exist in an environment intrinsically bathed in concepts of power. Consumed with his little self and his own importance, man often runs the risk of losing sight of the greater reality of a higher power and the opportunity it affords for spiritual growth, thus giving rise to the Rig-Veda quote, *Ego is the biggest enemy of humans.*

In relation to competition, the enlightened goal is not to strengthen the enemy ego, i.e., our ego is the enemy; nor expand its house of collyrium or well of poison. If we seek competition only to expand our ego, we're doing ourselves more harm than good. The goal of competition is to test ourselves, our skill, our character, our personal development. This is why we say, *we compete to test our skill, not expand our ego.*

Martial arts is a proving ground for the soul. Through it we acquire power, but what kind of power do we acquire - *Power in the Flock* or *Power over Ourselves*?

Power in the Flock is a reference to external, social power, the power that manifests itself over others. Power in the Flock is false, ephemeral and illusory. By exercising and exhibiting such power we become deluded, misguided, a detriment not just to others but also to ourselves. External power is false power.

Contrastingly, in having *Power over Ourselves* our concern is not in dominating others but in controlling our own mind, passions, ego and all the inner demons and dragons afflicting us from within. Inner power is true power.

Gautama the Buddha makes these relevant statements:

> *It is better to conquer yourself than to win a*
> *thousand battles. Then the victory is yours.*
> *It cannot be taken from you, not by angels or*
> *by demons, heaven or hell.*

> *Though one may conquer a thousand times a*
> *thousand men in battle, yet he indeed is the*
> *noblest victor who conquers himself.*

The irony of power is that the external version, the "power in the flock" variety, is an outward manifestation of inner weakness. Such an over-compensation often fools many people. Yet, upon closer scrutiny, those people who are boisterous, loud, vulgar, pushy, arrogant, imperious and overtly demanding are not powerful at all, but quite weak. Their bravado is nothing more than an attempt to gain externally what they lack internally - an integrated sense of self.

Martial arts is the perfect venue for exposing external power, which is really weakness, and developing internal power and strength. When people are intrinsically strong, they have no need to laud themselves over others. Rather, their way is to empower others, not disempower them. This is why *humility is the highest form of strength; arrogance the highest form of weakness.* Do we perceive Buddha, Christ, Kabir, Guru Nanak and other highly evolved souls to be weak? Quite the contrary. These were powerful souls with nothing to prove and everything to share.

As martial arts practitioners, students, teachers and competitors, we would be well-served to understand this difference between external and internal power and the competitive environment which tests us in relation to how we use power. It is not uncommon for some martial artists to use their martial prowess to intimidate, control and abuse others. It is a great tragedy, certainly for their victims but more for themselves because their power was given to them as a test to assess their worthiness to receive greater truths and, hence, greater power. When the power is abused, not only is their progress halted, but the karmic load involving the misuse of power becomes a burden to them. Eventually, they will be abused and controlled to the extent they abused and controlled others, either in this lifetime or a future lifetime. What we sow, we reap. What we place onto the Circle of Life, circles back to encircle us. We can't out run our karmas. In reality, we become the recipients or victims of our own making. If we place goodness onto the Circle of Life, then goodness circles back to us. Likewise, if we place meanness and wickedness on the Great Circle, then it is meanness and wickedness that eventually envelope us. There is no avoiding this truth. Therefore, we must be ever vigilant in our use of power, remembering that *we compete to test our skill, not expand our ego.* It is the ego that is the enemy, not the other guy. Once we conquer our own ego, we are well on the way to achieving the higher purpose of martial arts training - to integrate the body, mind and spirit.

#33

It Is Nothing To Begin.
It Is Everything
To Finish

It is not to disparage,

nor any seeker to diminish,

yet . . .

It is nothing to begin.

It is everything to finish.

Never run away from anything. Never! . . .
If you are going through hell, keep going . . .
You only have to endure to conquer.
Winston Churchill

Effort only fully releases its reward
after a person refuses to quit.
Napoleon Hill

Age wrinkles the body. Quitting wrinkles the soul.
General Douglas MacArthur

Most people give up just when they're about to achieve success.
They quit on the one yard line. They give up at the last minute of
the game, one foot from a winning touchdown.
Ross Perot

L ife is not only a journey, it's a test, a test to see if we can endure the struggles, trials, tribulations, heartaches, heartbreaks, tears, fears, and other incendiary challenges confronting us from cradle to grave. This test is meant to strengthen the soul for the journey ahead, not destroy it. If we give up, we fail. If we never give up, we triumph. It is nothing to begin this journey. We're born into it. However, it is everything to finish it. Therefore, we must never, ever quit.

As the esteemed Winston Churchill emphatically states: *Never run away from anything. Never!* He also encourages and admonishes: *If you are going through hell, keep going.* In many ways, Churchill was to Britain in their darkest hour what Lincoln was to America in her darkest hour. These were great and strong men without whose guidance, courage, wisdom and leadership the lives of untold thousands of people would have been drastically altered for the worse. They both knew they could never quit and didn't. They both led their countries through hell without stopping. They were blessed souls with powerful and meaningful destinies.

General Douglas MacArthur was a great military leader in the Twentieth Century. He understood quitting, and his quote hits the heart hard: *Age wrinkles the body. Quitting wrinkles the soul.* In other words, it's far better to have a wrinkled body, a wrinkled physical form, than to have a wrinkled, crinkled, crumpled and rumpled soul. The body is nothing more than structured dust. But the soul is that divine part of us that lives forever. It needs to be kept pure. Quitting adulterates it, leaving us unkempt, disheveled.

It's never crowded at the top of the mountain. Why? Because people quit the climb. Perhaps it's because the climb is hard, lonely, cold, daunting, dangerous. Whatever the reason, the reality remains that those at the top of any mountain, of any field of endeavor are few, and they are few because they never quit. But they are also the ones who gain the laurels and gifts of the climb. They, and they alone, are the ones deserving of the wealth of the climb, and only those who climb acquire such wealth.

True story. In a visit to Yosemite National Park in 1994, my daughters and I wanted to climb to the top of Vernal Fall. From the public road, the journey to the top of the fall is 1.5 miles. At .8 miles along the slightly elevating path is Vernal Falls Bridge. From there it's .7 miles to the top. As we started along the path, there were many people dressed in all kinds of attire. Some women were even in high heels. Hardly the kind of footwear to wear on a mountain trail. When we arrived at the Vernal Falls Bridge, there was a crowd. The path from there on was quite steep in relation to the path from the road to the bridge. At that point, most of the hikers quit the climb. But those who wanted to get to the top kept going, us among them. It wasn't all that tough a climb but it was more difficult than the first leg up to the bridge. For those of us who continued to the top of the fall, the reward was beautiful. Such a view! In simple fact, we who made it never quit. We kept going, enduring the slight discomfort of the climb. But because we never quit, we were among the ones who experienced the gift of the climb and the majesty of the view from atop Vernal Fall. Although this is a simple analogy, it underscores the value of not quitting and the rewards bequeathed on those who do not quit.

The Black Belt Book of Life   King

In more challenging struggles, however, the consequences of quitting can be perilous, even lethal. In a self-defense situation if we quit, we could easily lose our life. If, during family challenges such as the death of a loved one or loved ones, a divorce, bankruptcy or other heart-wrenching event, if we quit trying to maintain our psychological focus and emotional balance, we lose, and the consequences will most likely not be good. We must keep trying. There is no other alternative. How many people have quit fighting the urge to consume alcohol in an attempt to drown their problems, thus becoming alcoholics in the process? The same applies to quitting the struggle to stop the usage of nicotine and other drugs, thus leading to addiction and all of its attending evils? In quitting the struggle, such souls eventually become physically or lethally victimized by these consumptions and addictions. They suffer. Their loved ones suffer. To some degree, we all suffer.

Life is struggle. Great souls know this which is why they exhort us to keep fighting the fight and to never quit. As Churchill proclaims: *You only have to endure to conquer.* And isn't this the great challenge in life, to endure? Isn't this the way to lead a noble life, to endure? Christ said: *He that endures to the end shall be saved* [St. Matthew 10:22]. Need more be said?

And so it is for all of us in the journey of life or in any of its challenges or pursuits. *It is nothing to begin. It is everything to finish.* To finish, we must endure and never, never, ever quit.

#34

The "D" Line

In seeking patterns of success and a strategy to win,
The "D" Line offers five clear maxims:
Desire, Dedication, Determination,
Discretion, Discipline.

----

*A strong passion for any object will ensure success,
for the desire of the end will point out the means.*
Henry Hazlitt

*Desire is the key to motivation, but it's the determination
and commitment to an unrelenting pursuit of your
goal - a commitment to excellence - that will
enable you to attain the success you seek.*
Mario Andretti

*The question isn't who is going to let me;
it's who is going to stop me.*
Ayn Rand

*Discretion is the perfection of reason,
and a guide to us in all the duties of life.*
Sir Walter Scott

We all have dreams. But in order to make dreams come into reality, it takes an awful lot of determination, dedication, self-discipline, and effort.
Jesse Owens

Never give in! Never give in! Never, never, never, never - in nothing great or small, large or petty. Never give in except to convictions of honor and good sense.
Winston Churchill

Perseverance is a great element of success. If you only knock long enough at the gate, you are sure to wake up somebody.
Henry Wadsworth Longfellow

Nothing in the world can take the place of Persistence. Talent will not; nothing is more common than unsuccessful men with talent. Genius will not; unrewarded genius is almost a proverb. Education will not; the world is full of educated derelicts. Persistence and determination alone are omnipotent. The slogan 'Press On' has solved and always will solve the problems of the human race.
Calvin Coolidge

D eveloping success in any venture, especially becoming a Black Belt, doesn't just happen. Besides hard work and correctly applied effort, there are five principles beginning with the letter "D" that are key to success. They are: *Desire, Dedication, Determination, Discretion, Discipline.* Let's take a look at each of them.

1. Desire

Desire is the fire in the belly. It motivates us to move in a particular direction and engage in specific activities. Without desire, we would go nowhere. It is desire that sustains us. Whether that desire is to become spiritually illumined and free, a great martial artist, parent, teacher, writer, athlete, painter, mechanic, media reporter, contractor, lawyer, doctor, nurse, whatever. Desire is the fire that moves us in that direction.

2. Dedication

Dedication is devotion to the task at hand, a whole-hearted absorption in pursuing its manifestation. It is dedication that keeps our nose to the grind stone and our heart engaged. If we're to become a quality Black Belt, our heart, mind and spirit must be saturated with its achievement. The same goes for being the perfect parent, spouse, friend, business partner or leader. We must be totally focused on being the best we can be and making the appropriate sacrifices to achieve our goal.

If we're truly dedicated, we will sacrifice anything, even our lives if necessary, to fulfill our dreams. How many people, for example, sacrifice, have sacrificed, and will sacrifice their lives for freedom? How many will sacrifice their worldly pleasures for spiritual gains? How many parents will sacrifice their own dreams for the well-being of their children? How many musicians will sacrifice their time and social activities to spend countless hours practicing their art? How many teachers will give up their weekends for their students? On and on it goes. If we're dedicated to a cause, a person, a pet, a relationship, an ideal, a project or an activity, we will make the appropriate sacrifices necessary to nurture that dedication in order to manifest the goal which is fueled by our initial desire.

3. Determination

Determination is the iron will and heavy hammer, the relentless pressing forward until the goal is reached. When we're determined, we bite the bullet and march onward. If necessary, we even crawl on our bellies in mud and debris to reach our destination . . . but we never quit. Along the way we may have to endure incessant setbacks, enormous pain and seemingly endless suffering, tread water in an ocean of tumultuous tears set to the orchestral background music of sorrow-laden cries, chest-thumping lamentations and plaintive wails, but we press on because we simply and matter-of-factly refuse to quit, refuse to give in, refuse to suffer the indignity of failure and defeat. It is determination that makes us tough and daunting, a force to be reckoned with, a force that sets us apart from the "also-rans" and "couldn't-be-dones," a force that relentlessly persists and pursues its goals until it triumphs.

Calvin Coolidge was the 30th President of the United States of America. He stated a great truth relating to the virtues of determination and persistence which all of us would do well to emulate. His statement:

Nothing in the world can take the place of Persistence. Talent will not; nothing is more common than unsuccessful men with talent. Genius will not; unrewarded genius is almost a proverb. Education will not; the world is full of educated derelicts. Persistence and determination alone are omnipotent. The slogan 'Press On' has solved and always will solve the problems of the human race.

Calvin Coolidge

4. Discretion

Discretion is the ability to discern, discriminate, perceive and reason. By exercising discretion, we make choices between good and bad, healthy and unhealthy, wholeness-engendering or wholeness-obstructing. A wise man always looks ahead to the results of his actions *before* he executes them. A fool acts without thinking of the consequences of his actions and thereby suffers because of his lack of forethought. Sir Walter Scott, the famed Scottish novelist and poet of the 18th and 19th Centuries, offers this sage advice:

Discretion is the perfection of reason,
and a guide to us in all the duties of life.

5. Discipline

Discipline is the regimen, training and structure needed to insure success in any pursuit in life and, indeed, in life itself. Discipline is the crux of success. Without structure, without order, everything becomes chaotic and happenstance and goals don't materialize.

Becoming a legitimate Black Belt requires a strict regimen of study and practice for years. The word "legitimate" is used because in today's society there are those charlatans who peddle belts for a price to a stream of eager buyers desirous of skirting the required work in order to claim the prize without effort. Such individuals are only fooling themselves. They live in delusion, thinking that great skill can be achieved without the study, struggle, sweat, exertion, energy, and long-term devotion needed for legitimacy.

For those who are the "real deal" and who reflect the true nature of a legitimate Black Belt, their path is one of immense discipline. As discussed earlier, *there can be no excellence without effort* and it is discipline that sculpts that effort and creates a true work of living art in a living artist.

Don't be deceived. The Five "Ds" are necessary ingredients to success in life, as well as in the successful accomplishment of one's projects and goals in life. Embrace them. There is no other way to success.

#35

The "C" Line

In climbing high to reach nobility,
and supportive of their sibling Ds,
are the Cs of Character, Courage,
Commitment, Concentration and Consistency.

The first essential step to a spiritual life is character.
Saint Sawan Singh

Only a man's character is the real criterion of worth.
Eleanor Roosevelt

*The first prerequisite of a gentleman or a lady is a good
moral character. If that is not there, what else is left?*
Saint Charan Singh

Courage is the ladder on which all the other virtues mount.
Clare Boothe Luce

*Courage is rightly esteemed the first of human qualities... because
it is the quality which guarantees all others.*
Winston Churchill

The quality of a person's life is in direct proportion
to their commitment to excellence, regardless
of their chosen field of endeavor.
Vince Lombardi

Concentration and mental toughness
are the margins of victory.
Bill Russell

My ability to concentrate and work toward
that goal has been my greatest asset.
Jack Nicklaus

Consistency is the foundation of virtue.
Francis Bacon

Consistency, madam, is the first of Christian duties.
Charlotte Bronte

A consistent man believes in destiny,
a capricious man in chance.
Benjamin Disraeli

In any team sport, the best teams have
consistency and chemistry.
Roger Staubach

Continuing in the discussion of success in life and in our personal achievements are the five Cs, siblings to the five Ds. These foundational virtues are: Character, Courage, Commitment, Concentration and Consistency.

1. Character

Character is a virtue we build. Hopefully, we come into this life with good, even great, character. If not, and if we want to live a good and noble life, we must construct it, especially if we want to grow in the spirit. Furthermore, we must do this in spite of our failings. As Saint Sawan Singh states: *The first essential step to a spiritual life is character.* This is further corroborated by Eleanor Roosevelt's observation: *Only a man's character is the real criterion of worth.* Saint Charan Singh admonishes: *The first prerequisite of a gentleman or a lady is a good moral character.*

Building a strong character is like creating a garden. We need to plant the right flora, feed it, water it, and keep it pruned and properly cultivated. If we don't take excellent care of it, it will turn into a weed field, thereby losing its beauty. Character construction is a continual process in the making.

It's not easy to build and maintain a good character. This world is full of challenges, temptations, struggles. Being human, we're bound to stumble and fall at some point or another. As the saying goes, *Every Saint has a past and every sinner has a future.* Yet, if and when we fall, we must pick ourselves back up, clean ourselves up, examine why we stumbled and fell, make the appropriate corrections and then continue moving forward. To remain fallen is to deny our sincerity to grow. There is no disgrace in falling down. The disgrace is in not getting back up and carrying on. It's just like learning how to ride a bike, a horse or perform any other skill. We fall, we get back up, get back on, and get back getting on. It's a developmental process. We just have to keep working at it. Rome wasn't built in a day, nor are our characters. The thing to keep in mind, however, is that a good moral character is the goal if we want to reflect the excellence of life that we're capable of reflecting. Therefore, even though we may fall, we must not stay fallen. Giving up is a greater crime than falling down. Should we fall, as well we may, we need to get our bones, minds, morals, principles and spirits back up, make the needed changes, learn the needed lessons and press on because if we don't, it's a guarantee we'll never grow, never get better and never realize the kind of quality of character that is the hallmark of all great souls. Character building is a process, and in life, as in the path to becoming a Black Belt, the process is the product.

2. Courage

How many victories in life, how many blessings, how many opportunities have been lost for want of courage? As both Clare Boothe Luce and Winston Churchill declare respectively: *Courage is the ladder on which all the other virtues mount,* and *Courage is rightly esteemed the first of human qualities... because it is the quality which guarantees all others.*

Courage is being bold, fearless, intrepid, brave and resolute. It is the act of challenging our demons and dragons and not letting them control, limit, define or destroy our lives. Without courage, we would not stand up to the forces denying us or attempting to limit and dictate to us how we should live.

Courage, like character, is often a developmental process. Facing our fears, standing up to the bullies and bad guys in our lives, staring down our demons and engaging Goliath on the battlefield are how our courage is nurtured and sculpted. Little by little, battle by battle, shaky knee instance by shaky knee instance we grow until we eventually emerge from the Cocoon of Conquest a daunting and exalted hero.

Some people come by courage naturally. Others don't. This should in no way discourage anyone from learning to become more courageous. In martial arts, courage is developed by confronting an opponent in a controlled sparring environment and fighting him . . . all by oneself. Hopefully, this is done in a nurturing, safe and positive environment rather than through the school of hard knocks and street life. By learning to fight the fight by ourselves . . . alone . . . and not look to or rely on others for support or to fight our battles for us, we learn to be self-reliant, independent and courageous. It is probably one of the most satisfying accomplishments in a martial arts student's life to learn to have courage.

Going through such a transformation from tentative individual to courageous soul is a wonder to behold. Once courage is elevated to a meaningful level, the world becomes a totally different place, a place where one can walk freely without fear, maintaining a sense of confidence and dignity reserved only for those who have challenged and conquered the demons, dragons, rascals, rogues, goblins and ghouls of life.

The Black Belt Book of Life   King

3. Commitment

A commitment is a covenant, pact, promise, assurance, duty and obligation. If we have a desire to succeed or achieve a particular goal or condition in life, we must create a covenant, a promise to ourselves to achieve that end. If others are involved, than we must give an assurance to them as well. The thing is, we can't achieve success without commitment.

In this modern give-it-to-me-now world, commitment is becoming a rare quality, sadly. Yet, success and true achievement will never be realized without it. People may do their best to fool themselves and others, but in the end such gains will only be seen for what they are, hollow specters of illusion.

4. Concentration

This subject has been covered in the section, *Concentration is the first key*. Its power and importance in the process of success are mentioned here by two of the greatest athletes in their sports: Bill Russell, the famous basketball player with the World Champion Boston Celtics, and Jack Nicklaus, one of the most famous and accomplished golfers of all time. Russell declares: *Concentration and mental toughness are the margins of victory.* Nicklaus corroborates this statement saying, *My ability to concentrate and work toward that goal has been my greatest asset.* Need more be said? Concentration, it is a vital component in the process of achievement.

5. Consistency

If we're ever going to realize our goals, being sporadic will not get the job done. We need to be consistent and go through the often boring process of practicing our craft over and over and over and over and over again. Get the picture? We must be relentless in our consistency.

Francis Bacon's assertion that *Consistency is the foundation of virtue* is a worthy proclamation. Virtue is steadfast. It doesn't waiver. It is consistency - the activity of faultless regularity, that gives virtue its foundation. We could never rise to the level of being a Black Belt without it. Starting and stopping, and starting and stopping are lethal to the attainment process. If we're not consistent, we lose momentum and conditioning and therefore have to regenerate them. Doing so might work once or twice, but after a while such sporadic and intermittent behavior fail us. Ask any successful professional in any art and they will tell you that it is the daily practice, the ability to stay regular and consistent that is one of the great keys to their success. So should it be ours.

Thus, in summary of these last two sections, the five Cs - Character, Courage, Commitment, Concentration and Consistency, coupled with the five Ds - Desire, Dedication, Determination, Discretion and Discipline are critical essentials to our success in life. They are wonderful virtues we would all do well to emulate.

#36

The Learning Process

Learning is a process
that's challenging and fun,
comprised of three distinctive parts:
Acquisition, Integration, Execution

I am learning all the time.
The tombstone will be my diploma.
Eartha Kitt

When the student is ready,
the master appears.
Buddhist Proverb

I don't think much of a man who is not
wiser today than he was yesterday.
Abraham Lincoln

The ink of the scholar is more sacred
than the blood of the martyr.
Mohammed

L earning is a lifetime process. Because knowledge is infinite, learning will never end. To think we have ever come to the end, or will ever come to the end of the learning/knowledge spectrum, is unrealistic. This is why the famous singer, Eartha Kitt, said: *I am learning all the time. The tombstone will be my diploma.*

The learning process has three distinct parts:

1. Acquisition
2. Integration
3. Execution

1. Acquisition

Acquisition means to acquire. As a martial artist we acquire knowledge from classroom instruction, sparring with opponents, competing in tournaments, practicing, reading books, watching videos, sharing ideas with others and just plain observing all aspects of the art. So it is with any subject.

Yet, just because we acquire knowledge and gain information doesn't mean we have learned. It simply means we have obtained. Hopefully, the knowledge we've obtained is top-notch and instrumental in creating a foundation for our success as we move to the second stage.

2. Integration

This second phase of the learning process is where both the hard work and magic happen. It is here that we take the knowledge we've gained, incorporate and combine it into a workable whole.

The rub is that this phase is also the longest phase and, frankly, it really never ends because our learning never ends unless we choose to stop learning, especially if we're in a constant pursuit to achieve perfection in our chosen profession, art or skill.

This phase demands patience, persistence, determination. The acquisition part of the journey is often exciting because it's new, fresh and we're motivated. But the goal of mastery and perfection in the integration phrase takes seemingly endless time . . . and sweat . . . and effort . . . and struggle . . . and tears . . . and trying and more trying, a little success and more effort and on and on. But that's life. Anything worth achieving demands our greatest effort and integrative wholeness. It is in this phase that we learn that the process is the product, and if we're savvy, we learn to love and embrace the work.

3. Execution

This is the stage in which the results of our hard work and effort are realized. We gathered the information in the acquisition phase, honed it in the integration phase, and now in the execution phase we get to apply it and see the fruits of our labors.

This execution phase is the "do it" phase. We haven't learned anything until we can *do* the thing we're learning. Frankly, if we know something, we can do it. If we don't know it, we can't do it, whatever "it" is. To know is to do; to not do is to not know. We don't need to announce our ability in any field or in any skill. Our ability, not our words, will speak for us. It is this 'ability to do' that gives us confidence and sends a clear message that we have learned.

#37

The
Live-Evil
Riddle

Two sides to every coin
conjoined to form a middle.
Between the concepts "Live" and "Evil"
exists a secret riddle.

We are each our own devil,
and we make this world our hell.
Oscar Wilde

We make a living by what we get,
but we make a life by what we give.
Winston Churchill

There surely is in human nature an inherent
propensity to extract all the good out of all the evil.
Benjamin Haydon

There are only two ways to live your life.
One is as though nothing is a miracle.
The other is as though everything is a miracle.
Albert Einstein

Whatis the riddle between the concepts of *Live* and *Evil*? Within the two words there exists a secret enigma . . . and a powerful one. Do you know what it is? Can you figure it out? Look closely at the two words as they are placed side by side:

LIVE - EVIL

Do you see it? No? Let's adjust the lettering to give another clue.

Live - ɘviⅬ

How about now? No? Here's yet a different look. See it now?

Live - eviL

The riddle is that the word "Evil" is "Live" spelled backwards! Very interesting, isn't it? It is such a beautiful and profound observation, not just in the words' reversed spelling structure but mainly because the concepts and meanings of these words are exactly reflected in their configuration.

When we "Live" in the truest and highest sense of the word, we live in the atmosphere and move in the direction of all that is good, pure, positive, holy and divine. However, when we reverse direction and move instead toward that which is not good, impure, negative, unholy and demonic we, in effect, live backwards - the exact depiction of the spelling of the word "evil." In other words, when we move in a positive and divine direction, we *live*; when we reverse direction and go backwards, moving towards all that is negative and not divine, we commit *evil*. It's beautiful. It's true, and it's simple.

Some may argue that when we live we can perform actions that are both positive and negative. True. But when we reflect the *highest* condition of what it is to truly *live*, we manifest only that which is spiritual and divine and, therefore, if we reverse direction and go backwards, away from a positive direction, it is understandable that we engage in evil, i.e., we live backwards.

The moral of the story - move forward and *live*. Be positive in all you do, Climb. Seek higher truths. Elevate your mind, body, spirit and consciousness. Avoid reversing direction and moving in the opposite direction. Don't live backwards! Don't be evil. Don't turn the word *live* around and go backwards, committing *evil* in the process. Go forward. Live.

#38

The Secret of Greatness

In the realm of greatness
and all of its immensity,
the secret to its attainment
is the overcoming of adversity.

A great man stands on God. A small man stands on a great man.
Ralph Waldo Emerson

Responsibility is the price of greatness.
Winston Churchill

No man ever yet became great by imitation.
Samuel Johnson

Some are born great, some achieve greatness,
and some have greatness thrust upon 'em.
William Shakespeare

Forget about likes and dislikes. They are of no consequence.
Just do what must be done. This may not be happiness
but it is greatness.
George Bernard Shaw

Greatness references a degree of excellence and distinction that is extraordinarily outstanding and superlative. For those individuals, entities, events, circumstances and things that are truly universal, i.e. standing the test of time and culture, they are not unfamiliar to adversity. In fact, greatness is not acquired through the absence of adversity but rather in the overcoming of it.

Adversity is to greatness as heat, pressure and time are to the making of a diamond or as firing, folding and pounding are to the creation of a samurai sword. It's just part of the process.

Given this fact, we should not run from adversity, but challenge and embrace it, as any courageous warrior should. If we want to be good at anything, even be great, we must not only expect adversity but engage it, battle it, defeat it. If we don't challenge it, we can't overcome it and therefore we can't improve our self, our skills or our ability, let alone become great, if that's the goal.

What stand should we take in all this? Emerson's quote offers a clear platform: *A great man stands on God. A small man stands on a great man.* God is as great as it gets. It's only common sense that to be excellent in anything, to achieve the highest goal of all, we stand on God. Anything less, is exactly that, less.

#39

Price & Sacrifice

As the greatest gift exacts the greatest price,
the greatest accomplishment
exacts the greatest sacrifice.

Spiritual development requires great sacrifice.
Saint Sawan Singh

*Sacrifice, which is the passion of great souls,
has never been the law of societies.*
Henri Frédéric Amiel

*Great achievement is usually born of great sacrifice,
and is never the result of selfishness.*
Napoleon Hill

*Present your bodies a living sacrifice, holy,
acceptable unto God, which is your reasonable service.*
Bible: Romans - 12: 1

Everything in life has its price. In spite of what some people may believe, nothing is free, nothing. We simply must pay for everything we get in life. There are no free rides, no free gifts, no free admissions, no free drinks. Free "whatever" may be the appearance, but eventually the bill will come due and we will have to pay it.

Gifts have their prices, and the most expensive gifts bear the most expensive prices. Accomplishments have their prices, too, and *as the greatest gift exacts the greatest price, the greatest accomplishment exacts the greatest sacrifice.*

Sacrifice is surrender, a giving up, a renouncing, a relinquishing of something we value. The things we value the most naturally demand the greatest sacrifice . . . if we choose to surrender them. If we desire to achieve great things, we must be willing to pay the appropriate price and in doing so sacrifice greatly - of our time, effort, sweat, blood, tears, mind, comforts, luxuries, money.

Martial arts provides a worthy paradigm for continuing achievement and learning the lessons of price and sacrifice. If one wants to achieve an advanced beginner rank of Orange belt, for example, its achievement will involve a limited amount of sacrifice. Its value is relatively small from a martial arts perspective. However, if one wishes to achieve a Black Belt, its achievement will involve a much greater amount of sacrifice because it bears a greater price, a greater worth, a greater recognition. That price is years of dedication, devotion, determination, discipline, commitment, courage, consistency and so forth.

The greatest of the great understand this relationship between price and sacrifice. Do we not think that Abraham Lincoln was aware of the enormous sacrifice he was making in his service to his vision of a United States of America? Do we not think the great humanitarian, Albert Schweitzer, was cognizant of the price of his sacrifice in performing missionary work in Africa? And what about Mother Teresa? What of her sacrifices? Do we not think she was aware of them? And then there are the mystics and saints throughout history: Christ, Buddha, Mohammed, Guru Nanak, Kabir, Ravidas, Dadu, Tukaram, Swami Ji Maharaj, Charan Singh and others. These were souls of the highest order who not only understood the relationship between price and sacrifice but taught it, and more importantly, lived it.

It is true, as Henri Frédéric Amiel states, that sacrifice is the passion of great souls. Napoleon Hill confirms Amiel's statement with his own: *Great achievement is usually born of great sacrifice, and is never the result of selfishness.* Famous 20th Century Saint, Sawan Singh, instructs us that *spiritual development requires great sacrifice.* Without a doubt, if we want to achieve anything in this life that is associated with the term *great,* then we must be willing to endure the great sacrifice necessary to realize it. One does not buy a diamond ring with a dollar.

To this end we must not fool ourselves. True sacrifice is surrendering the things we value most. If we don't value something, there's no sacrifice in giving it up. If we don't like chocolate cookies, for example, and we say we're going to sacrifice eating them to loose weight, what kind of sacrifice is that? It's no sacrifice at all. It's pure self-delusion because we place no value on chocolate chip cookies. On the other hand, if we say we're going to give up eating meat because we want to lead a more spiritually compassionate life valuing all living creatures, even though we love eating meat, then that is a true sacrifice. It is a living sacrifice - living not only because the concept lives in us as part of a *living life philosophy*, but also because it supports the right of all living beings to live their own lives without the interference or predatory behaviors of others.

It does no good to fool ourselves by making false claims of sacrifice or in thinking we're sacrificing something when we're not. Others may be fooled but God won't be. So why go there? Why create illusions, let alone live in them? It's a useless and dangerous charade. We need to be honest with ourselves and then our sacrifices will also be honest, and in our quest to achieve, even become great or do great things, we will undoubtedly come to know the truth that *as the greatest gift exacts the greatest price, the greatest accomplishment exacts the greatest sacrifice.*

#40

Freedom and Oneness

To man God grants Divine Noblesse;
with Grace profound His children bless;
but the greatest gift of His Caress
is to merge into His Oneness.

He who is free from desires is richest.
Saint Sawan Singh

Only a virtuous people are capable of freedom.
Benjamin Franklin

No man is entitled to the blessings of freedom
unless he be vigilant in its preservation.
Douglas MacArthur

All differences in this world are of degree, and not of kind,
because oneness is the secret of everything.
Where can we go to find God if we cannot see Him
in our own hearts and in every living being?
Swami Vivekananda

Freedom and Oneness. They are arguably the two greatest concepts in the history of mankind, spanning eons of time and civilizations beyond measure. It is these two fundamental doctrines that conclude the forty philosophical vignettes of this work.

To live, breathe, move and make choices without interference, coercion, impediment or threat is to be free. How many people on the earth are blessed with such a condition? More importantly, how many souls have risen to the heights of spiritual liberation, totally immune to the constraints and shackles of the material world?

To abandon the mortal framework of the human body and its villainous ego and merge into the supernal ocean of the illimitable, omniscient, omnipotent and omnipresent power of God is Oneness. It is the ultimate achievement of the human form, the greatest blessing bequeathed on the soul in its journey through time and space.

Although these interpretations of Freedom and Oneness may seem esoteric, they are the immutable teachings of the highest order of Saints and Mystics throughout the existence of life on earth. Man can be free, not just in a worldly, political or cultural sense, but in a divine capacity, ascending to dimensions beyond the ken of human cognizance and perception. Such states of being are not easily attainable, quite the contrary, but they are real and obtainable to every soul who seeks to manifest their reality.

Martial arts is one system in the worldly milieu that serves as a vehicle in developing the individual's ability to pursue such lofty heights and begin the most miraculous journey and climb the soul will ever know, the journey to ultimately, and finally, free itself from a world that is foreign to its natural divine life and resplendent being.

What is it about martial arts that gives it this ability to serve such supernal ideals? It is because the ascent of the soul demands the application and manifestation of the exact qualities inherent in martial arts training: desire, dedication, determination, discretion, discipline, strength, sacrifice, character, courage, commitment, concentration, consistency, adaptation, flexibility, restraint, humility, the heart of a warrior, the ability to win and the resolve to ultimately triumph and realize its goals. In effect, martial arts training mirrors divine training. The process is the same. The difference is that martial arts training works at the lower level of worldly consciousness while divine training works within the scope and magnitude of the ascending, immortal consciousness. In effect, divine training is the next level up from martial training associated with the material world. The enigma is that such divine training is accomplished while living in the world. The only difference is in focus and goal orientation. The ideal is there. It simply awaits the definitive decision of the aspirant to embark upon its majestic journey. When the decision is made, unknown powers will come into play and personal intuitions of a more grand and spiritual scope will emerge to guide the soul inward and upward. One doesn't have to look. When the timing is right, the spiritual master, like the martial arts master, will appear.

CATALOGUE

OF

POEMS

&

QUOTES

POEMS & QUOTES
King

#1
Let your hands
give wings to your mind,
that you may find
an ever-greater Power of Life,
a Power preserving the
sanctity of your soul
and illuminating the radiance
of your Perfection.

#2
In your life journey from breath to death,
replete with all its possibility,
never forget . . . this is *Your Life*,
and it most surely is *Your Responsibility*.

#3
Attainment

As we progress and seek success
in its full embodied raiment,
Accomplishments are not our life,
our Life is our Attainment.

Possessions will not follow us
when we move beyond the grave.
Monies will be left behind
in the banks where they were saved.

Accolades and laurels
may, with some history, rest,
but none of these material things
will help us pass the Test.

Therefore, we should cogitate
on how our time is spent, for our
Accomplishments are not our life,
our Life is our Attainment.

How we live from day to day
at the center of our core,
is highly more important
than the things with which we score.

Ethics, morals, honesty,
purity, love and trust,
although not greatly popular,
are the things which go with us

when we move beyond this life
and the shadow of the veil,
for they will be the substance
of our life, its times and tale.

And they will be the basis
of the Judgment God will make
when He outlines the blueprint
of the future path we take.

Thus, prudent it would be to know
in quest of the Ascent,
Accomplishments are not our life,
our Life is our Attainment.

#4
Of all life's skills with which to carry,
remember this . . . *Balance is Primary*!

#5
Balance is Primary. This we see,
but in the struggle of life
Concentration is the very *First Key.*

#6
In the game of life, whether pauper, prince or king,
the fact remains --
To Become Everything We Must First Become Nothing.

#7

In cleansing the soul
and losing its dross,
it's axiomatic --
You Must Win The Cross.

#8

In a phenomenal world
with its contents illusory,
of all the triumphs
*Character Is More
Important Than Victory.*

#9

In the wisdom of time
with its messages ageless,
the pinnacle of all is that
Character Must Precede Prowess.

#10

Humility is the highest form of strength;
Arrogance the highest form of weakness.
As a silo sits vacant of fodder,
*A Black Belt Without Humility
Is Like A Well Without Water.*

#11

From dusk to dawn the world goes
circling sun with highs and lows;
within this journey Greatness knows
True Power Flows Not Shows.

#12

Action and reaction; Cause and consequence.
It is no mystery that
Competence Creates Confidence.

#13

Symbol before substance - pandemic renowned.
Symbol before substance - deluded clown.
Substance Before Symbol - turn it around.
Substance Before Symbol - deservéd crown!

The Black Belt Book of Life   King

#14
Within the heart emotions stir.
Failure is not what we prefer;
but yet, the victors all confer -
The Road To Success Is Paved With Failure.

#15
The meanings of strength are many,
but one thing is for sure,
in the struggle-strewn strife of life
Strength Is The Ability To Endure.

THE WALL

It stands, unyielding, to an ever-present flow of suppliants:
THE WALL

It beckons, calling and challenging those
whose spirit would be tested in the fire:
THE WALL

It rewards and holds within its bosom and on its face
those individuals who came to challenge and to conquer
and prove their spirit equal to the task:
THE WALL

It honors and presents forever to the world
those collective souls whose spirits would never die,
would never yield to the fire of its own relentless spirit:
THE WALL

It stands as a grand and noble legacy for grand and
noble conquerors - Black Belts of the Kiado-Ryu.
It is their exclusive right, their exclusive heritage,
their exclusive destiny.
It is undeniably and
unquestionably
their WALL.

THE WALL II

They have come in multitudes, for decades.
Through their sweat, blood, tears,
hopes and dreams they have come --
Seeking, striving to reach a pinnacle
only few have conquered;
Seeking to rise above
the mediocre and mundane
to stand apart in triumph!

But the Wall, standing as an edifice
to courage, determination and the
substance of a relentless spirit,
has broken all but just a few --
The few who could not be broken;
The few who would not be broken;
The few who can truly claim to be named
Black Belts of the Kiado-Ryu!

#16
In finding the mark and hitting it,
as we our goals pursue,
the key to raising the Cup is
Not To But Through.

#17
With any project you undertake,
to limit stress and insure progress,
the cardinal rule is simply this:
Preparation Is The Key To Success.

#18
We live in an age with effort waning,
with riches expected sans work;
but in all reality and actuality
There Can Be No Excellence Without Effort.

#19
In a world of slippery titles,
this truth to God we thank:
Rank Does Not Make The Man,
The Man Makes The Rank.

The Black Belt Book of Life   King

#20
In quest to master any art
and avoid unkind disaster,
it would be wise to recognize
Control Is The Mark Of A Master.

#21
Diamonds are made under extreme heat and pressure
over an extended period of time, not
by a mere and casual blowing
of an intermittent wind.

#22
In the journey of accomplishment
the wise this adage heed --
fast or slow is not of note,
of note is *Perfect Speed.*

#23
To not get drained and tired,
and not be madly dumb,
in all things great and small
we must *Maximum the Minimum.*

#24
Perfect Practice

Perfect practice, perfect makes.
Simple practice makes a habit.
If it's perfection we desire,
then we must make *Perfection* habit.

Simple habits, habits make.
The outcome of our loves
becomes extraordinary in the law
that *perfect is as perfect does.*

When we spend time in forming
those things we want in 'grooves',
then we must practice perfectly
for *perfect is as perfect moves.*

We can't expect perfection
from results our effort takes,
if we don't practice perfectly,
for *perfect is as perfect makes.*

Practice makes a habit.
Perfect practice makes perfect.

#25
Perfect Masters throughout time,
in all of their addresses,
state that in the mystic realm
Concentration Coalesces.

#26
From birth to death the truth be known,
when you cry tears
You're On Your Own.
If you're attacked when all alone,
the truth remains --
You're On Your Own.
Fair weather friends have always flown.
When your fame dies,
You're On Your Own.
So best to seek the sanctum
of the Journey headed Home
from this wasteland of the loveless
where *You Are On Your Own.*

#27
Life is full of problems,
and when they settle in,
remember, for solutions,
The Way Out is In.

#28
Living trapped within your self
certainly isn't savory;
Peace at any price is not peace,
it's slavery.

#29
In living life from birth to death
and in the filling of its cup,
responsible people realize that
Grown Ups, Own Up.

#30
In the day-to-day battles of life,
we can weep or laugh or cry,
but the indefensible truth
is that we either *Adapt or Die.*

#31
When confronted in life with options
and we wonder which option to choose,
there really is no other option:
Doing the right thing is the right thing to do.

#32
In the game of sport,
of competition and friendly foe,
We compete to test our skill,
not expand our ego.

#33
It is not to disparage,
nor any seeker to diminish,
yet . . .
It is nothing to begin.
It is everything to finish.

#34
In seeking patterns of success and a strategy to win,
The "D" Line offers five clear maxims:
Desire, Dedication, Determination, Discretion, Discipline.

#35
In climbing high to reach nobility,
and supportive of their sibling Ds,
are Character, Courage, Commitment,
Concentration and Consistency.

#36
Learning is a process
that's challenging and fun,
comprised of three distinctive parts:
Acquisition, Integration, Execution.

#37
Two sides to every coin
conjoined to form a middle.
Between the concepts "Live" and "Evil"
exists a secret riddle.

#38
In the realm of greatness
and all of its immensity,
the secret to its attainment
is the overcoming of adversity.

#39
As the greatest gift exacts the greatest price,
the greatest accomplishment
exacts the greatest sacrifice.

#40
To man God grants Divine Noblesse;
with Grace profound His children bless;
but the greatest gift of His Caress
is to merge into His Oneness.

QUOTES
General Authors

#2
Work out your own salvation.
Do not depend on others.
Buddha
[400 BCE]

I blame not another.
I blame my own karmas.
Guru Nanak
[15th/16th Century]

You are responsible for yourself.
You are not responsible for the world.
Saint Charan Singh
[20th Century]

#4
Anyone can teeter-totter
but not everyone can balance.
Anonymous

Man always travels along precipices.
His truest obligation is to keep his balance.
Pope John Paul II

The best and safest thing is to keep a balance in your life,
acknowledge the great powers around us and in us.
If you can do that, and live that way,
you are really a wise man.
Euripides
[480-406BC]

#5
Concentration is the secret of strength.
Ralph Waldo Emerson

#7
*Without recognizing the ordinances of Heaven,
it is impossible to be a superior man.*
Confucius

#8
The gem cannot be polished without friction.
Chinese Proverb

*Only a man's character is the real criterion of worth.
Do what you feel in your heart to be right - for you'll
be criticized anyway. You'll be damned if you do,
and damned if you don't.*
Eleanor Roosevelt

*Character cannot be developed in ease and quiet.
Only through experience of trial and suffering can the
soul be strengthened, ambition inspired, and success achieved.*
Helen Keller

#9
*The first essential step to a spiritual life is character.
One may deceive one's friends, relatives and even
oneself, but the Power within is not deceived.*
Saint Sawan Singh, 20th Century

*For he who is honest is noble,
whatever his fortunes or birth.*
Alice Cary

*Try not to become a man of success
but rather to become a man of value.*
Dr. Albert Einstein

An honest man's the noblest work of God.
Alexander Pope

#10
*We come nearest to the great
when we are great in humility.*
Rabindranath Tagore
[Nobel Laureate, Literature 1913]

To become truly great, one has to
stand with people, not above them.
Charles de Montesquieu
[18th Century French Philosopher]

If I have seen further, it is only by
standing on the shoulders of Giants.
Sir Isaac Newton

#11
Learn this from the waters:
in mountain clefts and chasms
loud gush the streamlets,
but great rivers run silently.

Things that are empty make a noise;
the full is always quiet.
Buddha

#12
Reason's whole pleasure,
all the joys of sense,
Lie in three words, -
health, peace, and competence.
Alexander Pope
[Essay on Man]

#13
Beware that you do not lose the substance
by grasping at the shadow.
Aesop

Be not deceived with the first appearance of things,
for show is not substance.
English proverb

The leader shows that style is no substitute for substance.
Lao Tzu

#14
Success consists of going from failure to failure
without loss of enthusiasm.

Success is not final, failure is not fatal:
it is the courage to continue that counts.
Sir Winston Churchill

Most people give up just when they're about to
achieve success. They quit on the one yard line.
They give up at the last minute of the game,
one foot from a winning touchdown.
Ross Perot

#15
You only have to endure to conquer.
Winston Churchill

What does not kill me makes me stronger.
Goethe

The strongest man in the world
is he who stands most alone.
Henrik Ibsen

Strength does not come from physical capacity.
It comes from an indomitable will.
Gandhi

Being deeply loved by someone gives you strength,
while loving someone deeply gives you courage.
Lao Tzu

#16
I can give you a six-word formula for success:
Think things through - then follow through.
Sir Walter Scott

#17
To be prepared is half the victory.
Miguel De Cervantes
[Author of *Don Quixote*]

Luck favors the mind that is prepared.
Louis Pasteur

Before everything else,
getting ready is the secret to success.
Henry Ford

If I had eight hours to chop down a tree,
I'd spend six hours sharpening my ax.
Abraham Lincoln

#18
Much effort, much prosperity.
Euripides

Success is dependent on effort.
Sophocles

The mode by which the inevitable comes to pass is effort.
Oliver Wendell Holmes

I'm a great believer in luck, and I find
the harder I work the more I have of it.
Thomas Jefferson

It is only through labor and painful effort,
by grim energy and resolute courage,
that we move on to better things.
Theodore Roosevelt

#19
Ranks of this world will not
be recognized in the next.
Guru Nanak
[15th/16th Century Saint]

High rank and soft manners may not
always belong to a true heart.
Anthony Trollope
[19th Century English novelist]

It is an interesting question how far men
would retain their relative rank if they
were divested of their clothes.
Henry David Thoreau

Fortune does not change men, it unmasks them.
Suzanne Necker

Uneasy lies the head that wears a crown.
William Shakespeare
Henry IV, Part 2, Act 3, Scene 1

Power tends to corrupt, and absolute power corrupts absolutely.
Great men are almost always bad men.
Lord Acton

No man is wise enough, nor good enough
to be trusted with unlimited power.
Charles Caleb Colton

Power, like a desolating pestilence, pollutes whatever it touches.
Percy Shelley

The boast of heraldry, the pomp of power, and all that beauty, all
that wealth e're gave, awaits alike the inevitable hour.
The paths of glory lead but to the grave.
Thomas Gray
Elegy Written in a Country Church-yard

Unnumbered suppliants crowd Preferment's Gate, athirst for
wealth and burning to be great; delusive fortune hears the
incessant call; they rise, they shine, evaporate and fall!
Dr. Samuel Johnson
Vanity of Human Wishes

All is ephemeral,— fame and the famous as well.
Marcus Aurelius

#20
*Only one who devotes himself to a cause
with his whole strength and soul can be
a true master. For this reason mastery
demands all of a person.*
Albert Einstein

*The happiness of a man in this life does
not consist in the absence but in
the mastery of his passions.*
Alfred Lord Tennyson

*All of your scholarship, all your study of Shakespeare
and Wordsworth would be vain if at the same time you
did not build your character and attain mastery
over your thoughts and your actions.*
Gandhi

*An appeaser is one who feeds a crocodile
hoping it will eat him last.*
Sir Winston Churchill

No man is free who cannot control himself.
Pythagoras

The process is the product.
Anonymous

#21
*We could never learn to be brave and patient
if there were only joy in the world.*

*Character cannot be developed in ease and quiet.
Only through experience of trial and suffering
can the soul be strengthened, ambition inspired,
and success achieved.*
Helen Keller

*Out of suffering have emerged the strongest souls.
The most massive characters are seared with scars.*
Kahlil Gibran

If I miss one day's practice, I notice it.
If I miss two days, the critics notice it.
If I miss three days, the audience notices it.
Ignacy Paderewski

If a dog walks through a cotton field,
he does not come out dressed in a suit.
Saint Sawan Singh

The whole world is overpowered by delusion.
The delusion is overpowered by none.
Saint Dariya of Bihar

#22
Impatience is wanting something to happen
before the due time.
Saint Charan Singh
[20th Century]

To every thing there is a season,
and a time to every purpose under the heaven.
[Bible: Ecclesiastes 3:1]

You win battles by knowing the enemy's timing,
and using a timing which the enemy does not expect.
Miyamoto Musashi
[Famed Japanese Swordsmen-16th/17th Century]

#23
There can be economy only where there is efficiency.
Benjamin Disraeli

The highest type of efficiency is that which can
utilize existing material to the best advantage.
Jawaharlal Nehru

There are only two qualities in the world:
efficiency and inefficiency, and only two sorts
of people: the efficient and the inefficient.
George Bernard Shaw

#24
Be thou perfect.
Bible - Genesis 17:1

Perfection is attained by slow degrees;
it requires the hand of time.
Voltaire

There is such a thing as perfection . . . and our purpose
for living is to find that perfection and show it forth.

The gull sees farthest who flies highest.
Richard Bach

God's work is permanent and everlasting
and exists in a state of perfection in every man.

Man is the top of all creation, the perfect handiwork of Nature in
all aspects. He contains within himself the key to unlock the
mystery of the Universe and to contact the Creator. It is the
greatest and the highest good fortune of any sentient
being to be born in the form of man.
Saint Jagat Singh
[20th Century]

Perfect is he who, by practice and meditation, lifts
his soul to its real abode, freeing it from all
bonds both internal and external, gross,
subtle and causal and thus detaches
his mind from the world and
its phenomena.
Swami Ji Maharaj
[19th Century Saint]

#25
If you don't concentrate, you'll end up on your rear.
Tai Babilonia

To be able to concentrate for a considerable time
is essential to difficult achievement.
Bertrand Russell

The stages of the Noble Path are: Right View, Right Thought,
Right Speech, Right Behavior, Right Livelihood,
Right Effort, Right Mindfulness and
Right Concentration.
Buddha

#26
The strongest man in the world
is he who stands most alone.
Henrik Ibsen

I am sure of this, that by going much alone a man will get
more of a noble courage in thought and word than
from all the wisdom that is in books.
Ralph Waldo Emerson

We must learn to live with ourselves,
independently of anything in this world.
Saint Charan Singh

I never must forget that none's my true
companion here, for all are
gathered here for selfish ends.
Saint Kabir

Regarding worldly relationship, it may be pointed out that all
relationships are based on selfish motives on this material plane.
Husbands, brothers, wives, sisters, other relatives and friends
are attached to us because of the advantages that accrue to them
from us and are apt to cool down in their zeal and love towards
us when they feel that we are of no use to them. Do not expect
much from them but do your duty towards them and care for
them even if they fail to reciprocate your love.
Saint Jagat Singh

Solitude
Ella Wheeler Wilcox

Laugh, and the world laughs with you;
Weep, and you weep alone;
For the sad old earth must borrow its mirth,
But has trouble enough of its own.
Sing, and the hills will answer;
Sigh, it is lost on the air;
The echoes bound to a joyful sound,
But shrink from voicing care.

Rejoice, and men will seek you;
Grieve, and they turn and go;
They want full measure of all your pleasure,
But they do not need your woe.
Be glad, and your friends are many;
Be sad, and you lose them all,—
There are none to decline your nectared wine,
But alone you must drink life's gall.

Feast, and your halls are crowded;
Fast, and the world goes by.
Succeed and give, and it helps you live,
But no man can help you die.
There is room in the halls of pleasure
For a large and lordly train,
But one by one we must all file on
Through the narrow aisles of pain.

#27
*We can't solve problems by using the same kind
of thinking we used when we created them.*
Dr. Albert Einstein

Every problem has a gift for you in its hands.
Richard Bach

No problem can stand the assault of sustained thinking.
Voltaire

Don't tell your problems to people: eighty percent
don't care; and the other twenty percent
are glad you have them.
Lou Holtz

#28
Better to starve free than be a fat slave.
Aesop

If slavery is not wrong, nothing is wrong.
Abraham Lincoln

No man is entitled to the blessings of freedom
unless he be vigilant in its preservation.
General Douglas MacArthur

The moment the slave resolves that he will
no longer be a slave, his fetters fall.
Gandhi

No man is free who cannot control himself.
Pythagoras

Without discipline, there's no life at all.
Katharine Hepburn

#29
Responsibility is the price of greatness.
Churchill

If you want to cut your own throat,
don't come to me for a bandage.
Margaret Thatcher

Let everyone sweep in front of his own door,
and the whole world will be clean.
Goethe

You are responsible for yourself.
You are not responsible for the world.
Saint Charan Singh

#30
The wise adapt themselves to circumstances,
as water molds itself to the pitcher.
Chinese Proverb

Fixed fortifications are monuments to man's stupidity.
General George Patton Jr.

The nature of war is ceaseless change . . .
It is one of the most important tasks of command
to effect timely and proper change of tactics.
Sun Tzu

All fixed set patterns are incapable of adaptability or pliability.
The truth is outside of all fixed patterns.
Bruce Lee

#31
Do what you should, not what you can.
Saint Charan Singh

The superior man understands what is right;
the inferior man understands what will sell.
Confucius

Do what you feel in your heart to be right - for you'll
be criticized anyway. You'll be damned if you do,
and damned if you don't.
Eleanor Roosevelt

He has honor if he holds himself to an ideal
of conduct though it is inconvenient,
unprofitable, or dangerous to do so.
Walter Lippman

#32
Ego is the biggest enemy of humans.
Rig-Veda

The world is a house of collyrium [an abode of evil];
a veritable well of the poison of egotism.
Guru Ravidas - 16th/17th Century Mystic

Learning increases ego instead of diminishing it
and takes us further away from the Lord.
Kabir - 16th/17th Century Mystic

Avoid having your ego so close to your position that
when your position falls, your ego goes with it.
Colin Powell, Secretary of State

It is better to conquer yourself than to win a
thousand battles. Then the victory is yours. It cannot
be taken from you, not by angels or by
demons, heaven or hell.

Though one may conquer a thousand times a
thousand men in battle, yet he indeed is the noblest
victor who conquers himself.
Gautama the Buddha

#33
Never run away from anything. Never! . . .
If you are going through hell, keep going . . .
You only have to endure to conquer.
Winston Churchill

Effort only fully releases its reward
after a person refuses to quit.
Napoleon Hill

Age wrinkles the body. Quitting wrinkles the soul.
General Douglas MacArthur

Most people give up just when they're about to achieve success.
They quit on the one yard line. They give up at the last minute of
the game, one foot from a winning touchdown.
Ross Perot

#34

A strong passion for any object will ensure success,
for the desire of the end will point out the means.
Henry Hazlitt

Desire is the key to motivation, but it's the determination
and commitment to an unrelenting pursuit of your
goal - a commitment to excellence - that will
enable you to attain the success you seek.
Mario Andretti

The question isn't who is going to let me;
it's who is going to stop me.
Ayn Rand

Discretion is the perfection of reason,
and a guide to us in all the duties of life.
Sir Walter Scott

We all have dreams. But in order to make dreams come
into reality, it takes an awful lot of determination,
dedication, self-discipline, and effort.
Jesse Owens

Never give in! Never give in! Never, never, never,
never - in nothing great or small, large or petty.
Never give in except to convictions of
honor and good sense.
Winston Churchill

Perseverance is a great element of success.
If you only knock long enough at the gate,
you are sure to wake up somebody.
Henry Wadsworth Longfellow

Nothing in the world can take the place of Persistence.
Talent will not; nothing is more common than unsuccessful
men with talent. Genius will not; unrewarded genius is
almost a proverb. Education will not; the world is full of
educated derelicts. Persistence and determination alone are
omnipotent. The slogan 'Press On' has solved and always
will solve the problems of the human race.
Calvin Coolidge

#35

The first essential step to a spiritual life is character.
Saint Sawan Singh

Only a man's character is the real criterion of worth.
Eleanor Roosevelt

*The first prerequisite of a gentleman or a lady is a good
moral character. If that is not there, what else is left?*
Saint Charan Singh

Courage is the ladder on which all the other virtues mount.
Clare Boothe Luce

*Courage is rightly esteemed the first of human qualities...
because it is the quality which guarantees all others.*
Winston Churchill

*The quality of a person's life is in direct proportion
to their commitment to excellence, regardless
of their chosen field of endeavor.*
Vince Lombardi

*Concentration and mental toughness
are the margins of victory.*
Bill Russell

*My ability to concentrate and work toward
that goal has been my greatest asset.*
Jack Nicklaus

Consistency is the foundation of virtue.
Francis Bacon

Consistency, madam, is the first of Christian duties.
Charlotte Bronte

*A consistent man believes in destiny,
a capricious man in chance.*
Benjamin Disraeli

*In any team sport, the best teams have
consistency and chemistry.*
Roger Staubach

Every Saint has a past and every sinner has a future.

#36
*I am learning all the time.
The tombstone will be my diploma.*
Eartha Kitt

*When the student is ready,
the master appears.*
Buddhist Proverb

*I don't think much of a man who is not
wiser today than he was yesterday.*
Abraham Lincoln

*The ink of the scholar is more sacred
than the blood of the martyr.*
Mohammed

#37
*We are each our own devil,
and we make this world our hell.*
Oscar Wilde

*We make a living by what we get,
but we make a life by what we give.*
Winston Churchill

*There surely is in human nature an inherent
propensity to extract all the good out of all the evil.*
Benjamin Haydon

*There are only two ways to live your life.
One is as though nothing is a miracle.
The other is as though everything is a miracle.*
Albert Einstein

#38
A great man stands on God.
A small man stands on a great man.
Ralph Waldo Emerson

Responsibility is the price of greatness.
Winston Churchill

No man ever yet became great by imitation.
Samuel Johnson

Some are born great, some achieve greatness,
and some have greatness thrust upon 'em.
William Shakespeare

Forget about likes and dislikes. They are of no consequence.
Just do what must be done. This may not be happiness
but it is greatness.
George Bernard Shaw

#39
Spiritual development requires great sacrifice.
Saint Sawan Singh

Sacrifice, which is the passion of great souls,
has never been the law of societies.
Henri Frédéric Amiel

Great achievement is usually born of great sacrifice,
and is never the result of selfishness.
Napoleon Hill

Present your bodies a living sacrifice, holy,
acceptable unto God, which is your reasonable service.
Bible: Romans - 12: 1

#40
He who is free from desires is richest.
Saint Sawan Singh

Only a virtuous people are capable of freedom.
Benjamin Franklin

*No man is entitled to the blessings of freedom
unless he be vigilant in its preservation.*
Douglas MacArthur

*All differences in this world are of degree, and not of kind,
because oneness is the secret of everything.
Where can we go to find God if we cannot see Him
in our own hearts and in every living being?*
Swami Vivekananda

BLACK BELTS
of the
KIADO-RYU

Founder & Grandmaster - Richard Andrew King

#	Name	Call Sign
1	Steven Ho	Widi
2	Jerry Gentry	Bones
3	Milt Jacobson	Super Zedha
4	Juliette Williamson	J. W.
5	Colin Lee	Semi
6	Bob Schreck	Grinder
7	Don Quinn	Quindar
8	Dan Asay	Basai
9	Rod Hickman	Rock
10	Eric Vind	E.V.
11	Ken Rogers	Ramjet
12	Rose Hoberg	Renegade
13	Genny Edge	Cougar
14	Greg Bendel	Maddog
15	Jason Brown	J. B.
16	Clark Hyman	Flash
17	David Shoemaker	Rhino
18	Jeff Kelly	Chainsaw
19	David Mooney	Nails
20	Doug McGregor	Doc
21	Kurt Hoberg	Raphael
22	Eric Tan	E. T.
23	Brent Berg	B. B.
24	Derek Berg	D. B.
25	Tim McCord	Thor
26	Geoffrey Huston	Eagle
27	Elizabeth Harkins	Panther
28	Jerry Alston	Shuto
29	Tim Huston	Chief
30	Jonathan Kuai	Poison
31	Jason Karuza	Buzzard

32	David Keith	Technician
33	Phillip Sampson	Ringer
34	Paul Daniels	Tron
35	Geoffrey Keith	Cazh
36	Chris Grau	Growler
37	Heather Corn	Burner
38	Lyle Peterson	Boomer
39	Steve Vertun	Coyote
40	Jeff Weber	Fireball
41	Vince Weber	Sly
42	Dave Sampson	Rugman
43	Taka Wada	Wadachild
44	Justin Brown	Great White
45	Steve Harrison	Shadow
46	Elizabeth Eckes	Quasar
47	Sergio Flores	Socco
48	Doug Krause	Pinky
49	Mike Watson	Pooh
50	Terry Bass	Slider
51	Todd Norman	Bufo
52	Thomas Lindsey	Draco
53	Adam Tichy	Cobra
54	Lee Murray	Strings
55	Anna Griffin	Wildcat
56	Pratik Patel	Cheetah
57	Tejas Maniar	Wolverine
58	Gwen Ryan	Hobbes
59	Greg Benedict	Earthquake
60	James Griffin	Psycho
61	Jeff Norman	Boa
62	Mike Benedict	Shooter
63	Kim Thomas	Cultivator

Black Belt Friends of the Kiado-Ryu

Bob "Trucker" MacFarlane
Lou Gacs
Linda Gacs

Richard Andrew King
~ Books ~
www.RichardKing.net

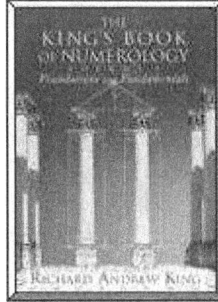

The King's Book of Numerology
Volume 1-Foundations & Fundamentals

The King's Book of Numerology, Volume 1-Foundations & Fundamentals provides complete descriptions of Basic Numbers, Double Numbers, Purifier Numbers, Master Numbers, the Letters in Simple and Specific form as well as the Basic Matrix, the numerological blueprint of our lives.

~

"*The King's Book of Numerology* series contains new information that informs and predicts more completely and accurately than any previously published numerological work. It brings back the empowered sciences of long ago, information long since lost upon this plane." ~ G. Shaver

"The best numerology book I've ever read." ~ M.W.

"I've learned as much about numerology from *The King's Book of Numerology* the last few days than I have in my past five years of study." ~ Frank M.

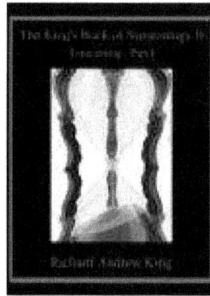

The King's Book of Numerology II
Forecasting - Part 1

The King's Book of Numerology II: Forecasting - Part 1 is dedicated to opening the door to the divine blueprint of our lives. That plan, that divine blueprint of destiny, is exact, precise, unchangeable, unalterable and . . . knowable, at least in general terms. Once this awareness of a predetermined fate becomes established through application of numbers and their truths, our understanding and consciousness of life will, no doubt, change. We will begin to see ourselves as part of an immense spiritual super-structure far beyond our current ability to comprehend, understand or perceive. Life will take on new meaning and, perhaps, we will even begin to awaken to greater spiritual truths. Subjects covered: Life Cycle Patterns, The Pinnacle/Challenge Matrix, Epoch Timeline, Voids, Case Studies and much more.

Blueprint of a Princess
Diana Frances Spencer - Queen of Hearts

The tragic death of Princess Diana of Wales - the most famous, the most photographed, the most written about woman of the modern world and possibly of all time - was one of the most shocking and saddening events of the late Twentieth Century. Not since the assassination of American President John Fitzgerald Kennedy in 1963, has such an event captured the attention of the world. On that ill-fated Sunday of 31 August 1997, and the following week until her funeral, there was much discussion and reflection of the Queen of Hearts, the People's Princess, England's Rose. But in all of the media news coverage, there was no discussion given to the cosmic aspects of her life and death. This book is dedicated to addressing those issues through The King's Numerology. Its purpose and hope is to offer some consolation and explanation as to that one question so poignantly written on a card of condolence left with the multitude of flowers before the gates of Buckingham Palace. . . "Why?"

~

"After learning from King's numerological teaching, it is impossible to conceive of going back to that 'twilight naive and foggy' state of being where one can only guess or hint at the truths, motivations and directions of one's life that is Pre-King. Not only do I recommend this book, but I suggest it and his other numerology books as absolutely necessary for the library of anyone even remotely interested in the science of numerology." ~ Hunter Stowers

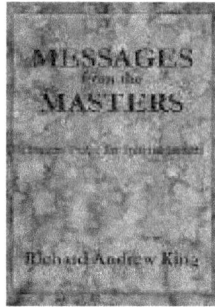

Messages from the Masters
Timeless Truths for Spiritual Seekers

In a time where there is more need for enlightenment than ever before, *Messages from the Masters: Timeless Truths for Spiritual Seekers* offers timeless truths for genuine seekers thirsty for spiritual nectar.

Masters are the Ph.D.s of the universe, the Light Bearers of the Divine Flame. Their knowledge and wisdom are supreme. They have no equal. Although appearing human, they are not. Masters are the exalted Sons of God. Their chief duty is to rescue souls, liberating them from the maniacal maelstrom and madness of the material world and returning them to their eternal Home with the Lord.

Messages from the Masters is a rich source of hundreds of quotes from a cavalcade of nine Perfect Saints throughout the last six hundred years: Guru Ravidas, Kabir, Guru Nanak, Tulsi Sahib, Swami Ji Maharaj, Baba Jaimal Singh, Sawan Singh, Jagat Singh and Charan Singh. The messages in this book focus on the importance of the Divine Diet, the priceless Human Form, Reincarnation, the World, the Negative Power and Soul Food.

Warning! *Messages from the Masters* is not for the faint of heart or the worldly-minded. Masters come into the world to sever our attachment to it, not make it a paradise. Although the epitome of love and wisdom, they shoot straight from the hip, pull no punches, favor no religion. Their universal message of soul liberation is reflected in the statement of Saint Maharaj Charan Singh: *Just live in the creation and get out of it*!

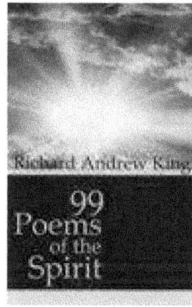

99 Poems of the Spirit

99 Poems of the Spirit draws from the writings of Perfect Saints, Masters, Mystics and Sacred Scriptures. Designed to lift the consciousness, mind and heart, all of the poems are original works by Richard Andrew King. Their purpose is to help connect the reader with the mystic side of life in order to enhance the process of self-realization while advancing on the spiritual path and climbing the ladder leading to the ultimate attainment of God Realization. It is a treasure chest of poetic spiritual gems offered to excite, educate and stimulate the mind and soul in the glorious journey of spiritual ascent.

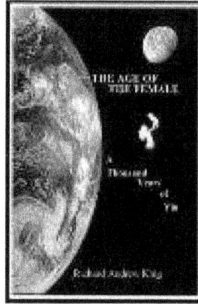

The Age of the Female
A Thousand Years of Yin

The Age of the Female: A Thousand Years of Yin highlights the profound and extraordinary ascent of the female in the modern world, placing her center stage in the global spotlight as presidents and leaders of nations, titans of industry, corporate executives, military generals, media magnets, doctors, lawyers and a whole host of other prestigious titles normally associated with the male. Why has her rise to prominence been so rapid, especially in consideration of historic time? Why also has there been an increased interest in other people's lives in our society, in competitive athletics, personal data collection and the exploration of space and other worlds? *The Age of the Female: A Thousand Years of Yin* answers these questions. It is an insightful and exciting read into these mysteries, offering compelling and irrefutable evidence through the ancient science and art of numerology that, indeed, the age of the female has arrived and the next thousand years belong, not to him, but to her.

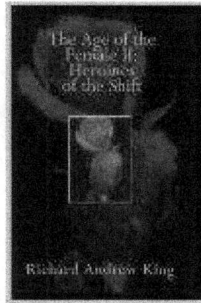

The Age of the Female II
Heroines of the Shift

The Age of the Female II: Heroines of the Shift continues the remarkable journey of the female's ascent in the modern world of the 2nd Millennium. This installment is a general read in five chapters honoring the accomplishments of women in categories of female firsts, female Nobel laureates, female athletes, female icons and female quotations. The achievements of the women featured in *The Age of the Female II: Heroines of the Shift* are deserving of respect and admiration. Their lives, challenges and successes are motivational catalysts for every individual to be the best he or she can be and to honor the very essence of what it is to be human. *The Age of the Female II: Heroines of the Shift* is intended to be an inspiring and educational read for everyone, not just women but men, too, offering knowledge and insight of the depth, power and daring-do of women as their Yin energy rises upon the global stage in this millennium which destiny has irrefutably marked as the Age of the Female.

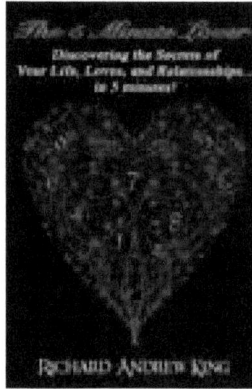

The 5 Minute Lover
Discovering the Secrets of Your Life, Loves, and Relationships in Five Minutes

Love. How powerful! How profound! Its majesty and sovereignty are unquestioned the world 'round. Love is the elixir of life, the apotheosis of its flame, the quintessence of human . . . and divine . . . alchemy. It is the fire of the heart and the inspiration of the soul. Of all the elements, ingredients and constituents of life, love is king.

We all need and desire love. Yet, how often has it eluded us? What are the secrets to finding love and making sure it's real, true and lasting?

THE 5 MINUTE LOVER reveals the mystery of love through the most ancient of all sciences . . . numbers, your numbers, calculated using only your full name and date of birth.

THE 5 MINUTE LOVER is based on thirty years of relationship research by master numerologist, Richard Andrew King. Applying his unique and revolutionary new theories, love and attraction between people can be determined using very easy to learn concepts. With a little study and practice, all this can be done in a matter of minutes.

Books Available At

www.RichardKing.Net

Contact

Richard Andrew King

PO Box 3621

Laguna Hills, CA 92654

----

www.RichardKing.net

www.Kiado-Ryu.com

www.KingsKarate.net

Richard Andrew King
Grandmaster, Kiado-Ryu
The Karate Institute of America [KIA]
[Founded 1979]

Richard Andrew King began his martial art studies in March of 1968 with the Tracy Brothers Kenpo Karate organization in San Jose, California, training with them for five years. Upon being transferred to southern California, he trained in the Ed Parker Kenpo Karate system and received his first degree black belt from Bob Perry, a first generation Parker black belt. Thus, King is a second generation Ed Parker black belt. In addition to being Grandmaster of his own system, King also holds a 5th Degree Kenpo Black Belt rating.

In 1979, King founded the Karate Institute of America in Orange County, California, and developed Kiado-Ryu Martial Arts, a well-rounded system consisting of basic medium style karate fundamentals, open hand forms, weapons forms, sparring, point fighting, street fighting, extemporaneous combat and philosophical principles of life.

Richard King's competitive career includes fifty-three championships at the Black Belt level in open competition, six All-Around Grand Championships (weapons - forms - fighting), a national #1 regional ranking in 1989 and 1993. His students have garnered four United States National Championships on the NASKA circuit, as well as amassing over three hundred first place victories in open competition.

www.ingramcontent.com/pod-product-compliance
Lightning Source LLC
Chambersburg PA
CBHW071934090426
42740CB00011B/1696